© DIS VOIR, 2023
1 Cité Riverin
75010 PARIS
www.disvoir.com

ISBN 978-2-38162-007-7

PETER GREENAWAY

FOUR STORMS & TWO BABIES

A LOVE STORY

CONTENTS

INTRODUCTION

A woman, restless for some meaningful experience in the search for love, meets a man in search of sex. They both take a chance of finding what they want and sleep together in a thunderstorm. The man falls in love; the woman falls for the sex.
The woman meets a second man and is intrigued. They sleep together in a second thunderstorm, and, knowing perhaps now how to do it, she falls in love; he falls for the sex.
A familiar eternal emotional triangle has developed.

In the presence of the woman, the men meet, quarrel and fight. The woman makes an uneasy peace between them. Through her the men become intrigued in one another. The woman knows she has a choice to make. Take love but not give it. Give love but not take it. She takes a chance to find love a second time. On her suggestion, all three sleep together in a third thunderstorm. The men are mutually attracted. They seek sex and maybe love with one another. The woman retreats, persuaded to drop out of the emotional triangle.

After the night of three-way sex, the woman discovers she is pregnant and decides to have the baby. She is not interested to know which of the two men is the father. The two potential fathers are invited to the birth of twins, two boys. The two men become fathers without knowing who is the father – two babies for two fathers. As a fourth thunderstorm approaches, the woman leaves for a distant country, still restless for some meaningful experience, leaving the babies with their fathers.

Peter Greenaway

PART 1

SECTION 1

FRONT TITLES- INTRODUCTION TO THE THREE PROTAGONISTS.
DAY. INTERIOR. AFTERNOON. SUMMER.

Each of the three major protagonists takes a shower in a generous space. Each of the characters is in a bathroom – three different bathrooms – in which through an open window we and they watch a summer storm with very heavy rain, but no thunder or lightning. The falling water of the shower inside and the rain falling outside against grey skies are all of a piece. There are wide shots, medium shots and close-ups – an extended essay of water falling on flesh. We are introduced to the three protagonists via their wet naked bodies.

THE TITLES ARE SUPERED OVER THE SHOWERING PROTAGONISTS.

FOUR STORMS & TWO BABIES

BY PETER GREENAWAY

Supermarket – late afternoon – Alan watches Patricia walk up and down the supermarket shelves looking for something. The supermarket is lit with harsh neon tubes regularly spaced above the shelving – we appreciate changes in the lighting as the actors move along the shelving. The camera tracks with them – often looking straight into their faces. There are super-close-ups of the food objects in their supermarket shopping-baskets and on the shelves with special attention paid to the writing of the food labels on the products and on the shelving. Indeed there is much attention paid in this film to typography, lettering and calligraphy. There will be super close close-ups of Patricia's handwritten shopping-list.

> ALAN
> So – what are you looking for? What can't you find?

> PATRICIA
> *(reading off a shopping-list in her own handwriting)*
> Tooth-paste, hair shampoo, balsamic sauce, green pesto, bean sprouts, white wine, a tin of baked beans, full fat milk, and oh - *(looking hard at Alan)* - love.

> ALAN
> A not unreasonable mixture, a little obvious to start with, then becoming xenophobic perhaps and even, I thought, exhibitionist, then heavy with saturated fats and then – well – just plain idealistic.

PATRICIA

I have idealistic tastes.

ALAN

And a very nice backside.

PATRICIA

Still early in the day for those sorts of
compliments, isn't it?
Bedtime is not until midnight.

ALAN

I see I have been rumbled.

PATRICIA

It wasn't difficult.
What's on your list?

ALAN

I don't keep lists. I'm an impulse buyer.

PATRICIA

(*she looks in his basket*) Chocolate biscuits,
frozen hamburgers, bottled beer, tomato sauce
and a plastic policeman. No green stuff – all
brown and red.

ALAN

Would you say – all the colours of shit and
blood?

PATRICIA

Crude and obvious? Masculine. And created
for someone living alone.
What's the policeman for?

ALAN

Keep me in order?

PATRICIA

Are you orderless?

ALAN

Moral order?

PATRICIA

Is that why he's plastic?

ALAN

Inferred snobbism about plastic is really old-
fashioned.
What are you - a hairdresser? A football
divorcee?

PATRICIA

As far as you're concerned I obviously could
own up to being both?

ALAN

Ah! I have discovered a sensitive soft spot?
When you have finished with your list, can I
have it?

PATRICIA

Don't you ever say please?

ALAN

Please.

PATRICIA

What do you want it for?

ALAN

To be a better shopper?

*Alan takes the list and looks at it. Handwritten list
backlit – lights shines through the paper.*

ALAN

I like the occasional alliterations.
Nice handwriting.
The Bs are a bit squashed.

PATRICIA

Then I have lost something else in this
supermarket?
*(mocking directive to herself – she looks along the
shelves)*
Look for un-squashed Bs.

ALAN

Only a graphologist would know and care.

PATRICIA

What's a graphologist?

ALAN

Someone who works in graphology?

PATRICIA

I am sure I am none the wiser.

ALAN

Don't worry too much. It is generally
considered a pseudo-science.
But I don't see love down on your list.

PATRICIA

Don't you?
I'm sure it's there somewhere.
Yes - there it is - look "love"

ALAN

That says luv - LUV – as in "Here's seeing you,
luv".

PATRICIA

You mix your accents, your quotes and your
chauvinisms.
And you're wrong - it says lav - LAV
Short for lavatory paper.

ALAN

From love to lavatory paper is a steep hill.
Up or down?

PATRICIA

I am really not sure. *(tears in her eyes which he
sees)*

ALAN

I tell you what - *(quickly as though afraid of losing
the moment of opportunity)* - why don't I pay for
yours and you pay for mine and whoever is the
least expensive, buys coffee next door, see you
there in five minutes, don't be late.

SECTION 3

CAFÉ CONVERSATION
Day. Interior. Evening. Summer.

Cafe – early evening – still daylight – approaching magic-hour - they sit side by side at a window at a table in a modern café, drinking cappuccinos, overlooking the busy street where there are poster-advertisements with copious lettering, and some bright flickering neon-letters. She is noticeably silent and looks out of the window. The major light source is the street and its activity. Occasional car headlights flick across them through the plate glass window, and then their faces are occasionally lit by the red tail-lights of cars.

ALAN
Are you in a hurry?

PATRICIA
I wasn't.

ALAN
But you want to be now?

PATRICIA
Not necessarily.

ALAN
The stimulus of shopping freed your tongue.
Now you're mostly silent.

PATRICIA
Mostly? I thought I was completely silent.

ALAN
Your breathing's heavy.

PATRICIA
Sorry. I'll stop breathing.

ALAN
Won't be necessary.
(a long pause)
Very well. You win.
I know what baked beans are, but what on earth is love?

PATRICIA
Don't be hasty. Do you really know what baked beans are?
Where they come from? Who planted them?
Watered them, harvested them, washed them?
Put them in a can with salted sauce?
Put the salt in the sauce? Stirred the sauce?

ALAN
What are you now - advertising agency, cook, nutritionist?

PATRICIA
The tin needs a label.

ALAN
Don't tell me this is where we need a graphologist?

PATRICIA
If I microwave the beans on toast …

ALAN
Don't ask me who baked the bread?
Who made the knife?
You have beautiful teeth.
Who is your dentist?

PATRICIA
Love - you see - like baked beans, is not so simple.

ALAN
So up or down?

PATRICIA
Pardon?

ALAN
In love.
Are you climbing up or falling down?
It's always one or the other.

PATRICIA
No it isn't. I am waiting.

ALAN
But not with any enthusiasm, and not with much joy.

PATRICIA
You saw my list. I am looking to buy some love.

ALAN
I could sell you some.

PATRICIA
How expensive is it? Is it the genuine item?
Will it be the real thing?
Do I get my money back if unsatisfied?
My dignity back if unsatisfied?
Hope back if unsatisfied?

ALAN
Of course.

PATRICIA
No additives? Sugar content?
Will I become overweight on your love?

ALAN
This food and love stuff is sort of confusing.
It could bring on indigestion?

PATRICIA
You are what you eat. Are you what you love?

ALAN
My God your worldly wisdom is turbulent.

PATRICIA
It's all merchandising. Exchange. Negotiation.
Barter.
I want this, you want that.
In the market place there is no such thing as a free lunch.
In the world in general there is even no such thing as a free smile.
I don't believe in altruism or philanthropy.
So against the odds, how can we make love work?

ALAN
I'm impressed.

PATRICIA
(looking troubled) I've been thinking about it for a long time.

ALAN
Well - you know that I am not going to pay you for it in any true financial sense.
That could be prostitution.
You might get some flowers or a meal.

They used to include chocolates at times like this, but that's now unacceptable.
We could manage a trip to the movies, though I don't like cinema very much, in fact, not at all.
Sharing your emotions in the dark with a bunch of strangers.
We could start by trying a drink after dark.
Love often looks better with a little alcohol and a little artificial light.

PATRICIA

Hey I'm looking, not searching.

ALAN

But I get the impression you've gone beyond the window-shopping stage.
And I want something in exchange.
Even looking at me instead of looking out of the window would be a start.

SECTION 4

CONVERSATION AT THE BAR

Day. Interior. Late Evening. Summer.

Bar - evening – still just light - they sit at the bar on stools. They are variously lit by changing coloured neon advertising signs in the bar. A television above the bar with a low soundtrack shows a weather forecast which is largely text and diagrams anticipating rain and storms. There are moving weather maps in lurid colours due to the TV's poor visual tuning.

ALAN

So – if I try to give you love - I want something in exchange.

PATRICIA

Would that be a baby?

ALAN

A baby!? Jesus! You are working quickly. You want a baby?

PATRICIA

That made you jump, didn't it?
And Jesus is a good example. There are lots of images of the baby Jesus about.
Isn't that what it's all about?
Making babies?
We're conditioned. I'm conditioned. You are certainly conditioned.

ALAN

Is it that obvious?

PATRICIA

Yes, it is. Yet another man eagerly scattering seed.

As soon as you see an eligible woman – you
start wanting to scatter seed.
However, you rarely want the consequences.
You want sex and I want love.

ALAN

Could that be the basis for a contract?

PATRICIA

I can guarantee the sex, but you can't guarantee
the love.

ALAN

You're right of course. At our age.

PATRICIA

Our age?

ALAN

We've all gone beyond the window-shopping.
Except you of course - you still think
favourably of the super-market.
Oh dear, you're distracted.
Looking out the hypothetical window again.

*She finishes her wine, looks at her watch and makes
moves to leave.*

ALAN

Oh dear, oh dear.
I'm reading the signs.
In the supermarket, you are noisy, interested,
curious, witty.
Then after reflection, twenty minutes later, in
the café, you are bored and cynical. Then you
decide in the bar – that it isn't going to work at
all.
Three goes at it.

I admire your staying power.
I am not the right bargain, am I?
Just practically - you need not go so very deep,
and we've only just met
and it's today, a long way to go till the weekend
- and the bruising can be bandaged by
tomorrow afternoon.
So - what's so wrong about me?
Wrong haircut? Wrong accent? Wrong
approach?
Too talkative?
Too old even?
Too talkative for one so old even?
I am 33. Age of Christ and Alexander at death.
They may even have been the same person.

PATRICIA

Do you think so?

ALAN

Handsome?

PATRICIA

Was Christ handsome?

ALAN

Energetic? Ambitious?

PATRICIA

Ambitious? Was Christ ambitious?

ALAN

He wanted to convert the world.

PATRICIA

Do you and Christ want to conquer the world?
I can't of course tell if you are telling the truth,
But as far as Christ is concerned - that's not
quite what I was taught.

ALAN

Accidental death.

PATRICIA

Really? Christ had an accidental death?

ALAN

Alexander. He died of a mosquito bite.

PATRICIA

I thought that was Byron?
It's curious – suspecting that we are both non-
Christian – how often Christ pops up.
Even invoked when we swear. You swear a lot.

ALAN

Do I?

PATRICIA

But you're alright. You're doing good.
Alexander and Byron both happened in Greece
– so you're close.

ALAN

Byron? Hey – ambidextrous? That was slow of
me.
So, maybe I'm the wrong sex for you.

PATRICIA

No. We wouldn't have got this far if that was
the issue.

ALAN

Well if it was, I wouldn't have minded wearing
a skirt to watch you brush your teeth in a white
tiled bathroom somewhere in the suburbs.

PATRICIA

Really?

ALAN

Well - there would have to be a cold beer in the
fridge.

PATRICIA

You bought the beer in the supermarket.
I have a fridge.
And we will have to take a tram.
Is that suburban enough for you?

PART 2

SECTION 5

APARTMENT BATHROOM.
Late evening into Night. Interior with Exterior View. Fifth Floor.
Thunderstorm. Summer.

Patricia's bathroom in her flat. Late evening. They are
standing in front of a bathroom mirror over a sink.
Double reflections. There is an open window in the
bathroom overlooking the city where there is still some
day-light but the evening lights are coming on. Patricia
is brushing her teeth – and with her mouth full of
toothbrush and toothpaste – cannot speak – she nods
her responses. Alan is wearing a kitchen apron over his
trousers. They are largely lit from above. The suburban
bathroom light is poor.

> ALAN
>
> Well, it must be said, we've come a long way
> in four short steps.
> Supermarket, coffee-shop, bar and suburban
> bathroom.
> And it's now dark and there's lots of artificial
> light about - perhaps too much.

He switches off the light over the sink. A slice and sliver
of light diagonally illuminates Patricia's head and face.
Looking at his darkened reflection in the mirror Alan
pats his hair.

> ALAN
>
> If you don't like my hair, you could cut it for
> me.
> Wash it even?
> I always thought that washing someone's hair

was pretty sensuous and caring and of course
useful.
Are you in fact a hairdresser? That is if you are
not a footballer's ex-wife?
Washing my hair. Could it possibly be a step
towards love?
Tell you what? You go and make the baked
beans on toast.
I'll take a shower and wash my hair.
And then we can drink your Australian
Chardonnay.
And discuss what we have in common - if you
like?

SECTION 6

APARTMENT KITCHEN AND BATHROOM
Night. Interior. Thunderstorm. Summer.

*In the very small kitchen across from the small
bathroom, the advertised roles are reversed. Alan
prepares the snack and opens the wine whilst Patricia
undresses and showers, washing her hair. They talk
across the corridor between kitchen and bathroom in
the small flat. There are small Matisse "Interior/
Exterior" reproductions framed and hanging on the
wall.*

ALAN
You know this sounds bad.

PATRICIA
What does?

ALAN
I am in your kitchen baking beans on your toast
- and I don't know your name.

PATRICIA
What's so terrible about that?
Kitchens don't demand names.
And I'm happy to stay anonymous for now.

ALAN
So you're not going to tell me?

PATRICIA
Not yet.

ALAN
"Not yet" sounds as though it has a future.
So have we started on a journey?

PATRICIA
We'll see.

ALAN
A short journey to first base?

PATRICIA
First base? Is this going to be a game or a
military exercise?

ALAN
Depends on your technique.

PATRICIA
Technique? Do I have technique?
All sounds very manipulated.
What happens next?

ALAN
I am making us something to eat.

PATRICIA
We could lay it on the balcony table.

ALAN
You don't have enough room in this kitchen to
swing a cat,
but you do have a balcony?

PATRICIA
Sure. I need a taste of the open air at all times.
Interiors, exteriors.
Otherwise I would drown.

*From the kitchen, he watches tantalising glimpses of
her naked buttocks visible round the edge of the
shower-curtain.*

SECTION 7

APARTMENT BALCONY
EVENING/NIGHT. INTERIOR WITH EXTERIOR VIEW. THUNDERSTORM.
SUMMER.

Balcony overlooking the dark city. They eat their frugal
snack in the semi-darkness on the small balcony of
Patricia's small flat as a storm approaches - their faces
lit by candles that are blown by the wind of the coming
storm. We watch them from the small dining room
looking out, and we watch them from outside looking
in. We are very aware of Interiors and Exteriors.

PATRICIA
I like windows.
Framing the view.
I like being up high. It means I can throw my
glance.
"Over the hills and far away".
I have always liked that phrase.

ALAN
No hills to be seen. This country has a
reputation for being very flat.

PATRICIA
Hypothetical hills.
With my glance like a torch-light.

She holds her head stiffly and placing both hands either
side of her brow, she swivels her head; she pretends her
head is a search-light swinging round the horizon.

ALAN
The only thing cinema invented they say was
the gance - glance.
Very Able.

The usherette's torch.
You don't get usherettes any more – do you?

PATRICIA
For someone who doesn't like cinema it occurs
remarkably often in your conversation.

ALAN
No hills - but thunderclouds. Sweeping in from
the Atlantic.
Can I hear thunder?

They both can hear distant thunder.

PATRICIA
That's exciting – don't you think?
I need a visit to those hypothetical hills.
I am going on a long journey some day.

ALAN
Sounds sad.
What has kept you so far?

PATRICIA
I need to find out some things and then I can go
travelling.

ALAN
What do you need to find out?

PATRICIA
What it's all about?

ALAN
You strike me that you know a lot about what's
it's all about already.

PATRICIA
Getting up in the morning.

ALAN

Going to work?

PATRICIA

Working?

ALAN

Going home?

PATRICIA

Washing your hair?
Going to bed, sleeping, dreaming.

ALAN

The usual.
Sounds very grey.

PATRICIA

Only if you are colour-blind.

ALAN

Does dreaming come with you then at the very
end of the list?

PATRICIA

Supermarket, café, bar, cinema, dreaming.

ALAN

I hate the cinema.

PATRICIA

We know. You've told us.

ALAN

Too much dreaming.

PATRICIA

What have you got against dreaming?

ALAN

Treacherous. I want to end up with the real
thing.
Dreaming can get in the way and become a
substitute.
I think dreaming should be done when you are
asleep.
Then it's random.
Outside your control.
And that sort of dreaming is done in bed.
Do you have a bed?

PATRICIA

I do. And you've seen it.

ALAN

How about using the bedroom for making some
dreaming?
If I were you I would hope to have some bright
flashes in the grey.
We could do that perhaps in your bedroom?

Flashes of lightning in the distance.

ALAN

There you go then – flashes of light in the grey.
With some thunder.

PATRICIA

If you like.

ALAN

We could hope for some thunder.

PATRICIA

Thunder for the sex? Lightning for the love?

ALAN

Are you drunk?

PATRICIA

Are you kidding?
Perhaps I ought to be.
It's the stimulus of being up high with a storm coming.

APARTMENT BEDROOM UNDRESSING
Evening/Night. Interior with Exterior View. Thunderstorm. Summer.

The balcony gives onto the bedroom. With the storm approaching and lightning flickering and lighting up Alan and Patricia in her bedroom – they undress prior to going to bed to make love. Pictorial emphasis on interiors and exteriors.

ALAN

Now that there's a thunderstorm coming – have we decided to go to bed?

PATRICIA

Let's see.
Depends on the approaching storm.

ALAN

Are you afraid of storms?

PATRICIA

Ordinarily no.

ALAN

On the whole, despite your doubts, I think you're courageous.

PATRICIA

How's that?

ALAN

You got us here.
All the way.

PATRICIA

Satisfied?

ALAN

Depends on what happens next.

They sit in their underwear on the edge of the bed
facing the window, the balcony and the coming storm.
We see them from the rear and from the front.

PATRICIA
Well it looks as though a thunderstorm happens
next.
Should we just lie down and enjoy it?

ALAN
Well - we could be prepared?

PATRICIA
Well - I am thoroughly washed.
And I hope you are.
Sweet armpits.

ALAN
Clean navel. Clean feet.

PATRICIA
Clean vagina. No unexpected tastes.

ALAN
Hey – that could be an invitation? Oral sex?

PATRICIA
No faecal leakages.

ALAN
Hey - am I understanding your preferences?

PATRICIA
What about you?

ALAN
Washed prick.
Clean anus. Clean ears. Even super-scrubbed
teeth.

PATRICIA
A mouth ready for kissing?
What about your mind? What's that ready for?

ALAN
Well to be honest - my mind is not so clean.
I am dreaming that you are - as they say - going
to be a drunken angel in bed.

PATRICIA
That's full of problems.

ALAN
Why?

PATRICIA
It was you who did the drinking.

ALAN
I did not drink so much.
I drank beer, you drank wine.
Takes more beer than wine to get receptive.

PATRICIA
Receptive to what?

ALAN
Angels?

PATRICIA
Angels are sexless and they don't sleep.

ALAN
Ever?

PATRICIA
Ever.
And they don't have navels.
I have a navel – look.

She shows him.

ALAN

Nipples? Do you have nipples?

PATRICIA

Yes. Absolutely. Two of them. Curious isn't it.
One would do.

*Showing him her nipples. They both look at her nipples
with great interest. Alan goes to touch them – Patricia
stops him.*

ALAN

Well two nipples are useful if you are thinking
of having twins.

PATRICIA

In an angel – they are non-functioning in any
real sense and only to complete the simulacrum
of looking human.
Little Gods made in His image.

ALAN

You are very well informed.
Where on earth did you pick up all this
theological stuff?
It's too advanced for me.

PATRICIA

My father's a priest.

ALAN

God!?

PATRICIA

Exactly. Yes - God.

Patricia watches Alan's face.

PATRICIA

Well - you haven't left. God's normally a test
that sends them away.

ALAN

Sends who away?

PATRICIA

The faint-hearted.
God is considered a prick-dropper.

ALAN

Could be the contrary - could be to my
advantage.

PATRICIA

Why?

ALAN

Having a priest for a father could suggest
innocence.

PATRICIA

Innocence because my father sells God?

ALAN

Are we back to supermarkets?

PATRICIA

A church is a sort of supermarket.
Cathedrals are sort of super supermarkets.
Many exchanges of a financial nature happen
in a cathedral.

ALAN

The cathedral as a bank?

PATRICIA

And your reaction of course - conventionally -
is also very insulting,
very condescending, and very patronising.

ALAN

I can see why.

PATRICIA

Well that's good.

ALAN

Implies that I want to seduce an innocent.

PATRICIA

Well perhaps you could succeed in your dreams and hopes.
(mocking) Imagination is very very important in these things.
It's almost always better in the head than in the bed.

ALAN

Don't tell me you're a virgin?

She laughs.

PATRICIA

No - I lost that piece of protective gristle a long way back.
But I can very safely say I am an innocent in love.
I am even a virgin in love - if that helps.
I've reached the age of Christ and Alexander at death,
And the age I will be in Heaven, according to Saint Augustine.
And I have not really experienced love, real love.
There have been various feints and compromises, half-turns, phantoms and subterfuges, and quite a number of would-bes and wannabes.

ALAN

Sounds like a great deal of practice.

PATRICIA

Yep! I tried hard. Too hard maybe.

Crash of thunder.

ALAN

Storm's getting closer.
Are we - you and I - getting closer to whipping up a storm?

PATRICIA

So - if you like – if it helps you – you could think of me as a virgin.

ALAN

I'll try. And I'll enjoy trying.

PATRICIA

It might help you get an erection.

ALAN

I have one already- look.

He stands up and stands before her, and takes off his underpants. She is curious.
They both look at his erection. He is well endowed. He has an erect prick lit by lightning.

ALAN

I have had one all evening.
But it was your teeth that did it.
I just had to imagine you biting my prick.

PATRICIA

Masochist?

ALAN

Are we going to experience such masochism now?

PATRICIA

Who knows - kiss me.

He sits on the bed. They kiss on the mouth. And then part.

ALAN

I like the taste of your toothpaste.
But it could have also been the sight of your backside.
I saw your backside in the shower just now.

PATRICIA

Is that why the toast was burnt?

ALAN

Trying kissing me again. I enjoyed it.

They kiss again – more sensuously – exchanging saliva.

SECTION 9

APARTMENT BEDROOM - ON THE BED
Night. Interior with Exterior View. Thunderstorm. Summer.

They are both lying naked side by side under a sheet on the bed. Profiles with the balcony beyond and the storm.

PATRICIA

I am an amateur.
I am an amateur human being.

ALAN

Oh?

PATRICIA

I want to be a professional - really join the human race.
Use up all my potential.
Do everything that my mind and body was made for.
I aim to be a very professional human being.
I have fooled around for too long.
And I don't want to find out that looking for love was a big and probably unnecessary detour on the way to death - a fool's errand.
There must be countless millions of other ways to live.
I want to live some of those other ways.
I live probably five ways at most.
Single woman, rent-payer, office-skivvy, my mother's daughter,
full-time screen watcher …

ALAN

Doesn't the rest of the world live the same way?

PATRICIA

No - it does not. Far more options are available.
I am 33 - I have fifty years to look around.

I have till I'm eighty - not so long.
Nobody produced much after their eightieth birthday unless they had produced something significant before.
Then I can die a professional human being - used up.
Imagine only two sips out of a whole cellar of good wine.
Three pages out of a library of ten thousand books.
Three handshakes in a very crowded airport.
That's all I have had.

ALAN

Could be more than enough - it strikes me.
One should go for quality rather than quantity.

PATRICIA

One self-generated fart in a world of smells.

ALAN

More than more than enough.

PATRICIA

Twenty passionate kisses on the mouth in ten years.

ALAN

Come on –

PATRICIA

Ten passionate kisses on my cunt in as many.
That's all it's really been.
Metaphorically, symbolically - yes - damn it - yes.

In something like anger she throws the bed-sheet off their reclining bodies.
Alan is revealed to have been playing with his erect prick under the sheet – he does not stop. Patricia has been playing with her erect nipples – she does not stop.
They have both been anticipating love-play.

PATRICIA

You know - when people say they have hundreds of friends – it's just not true – when they say they have seen thousands of films – it's just not true – one film every night for two and half years is still not a thousand films – that they read thousands of books – it's just not true. How long does it take you to read a decent novel – a week? – that's only fifty-odd a year – not at all so many.
Most people don't remotely live a life - they tinker about – most people are amateurs.

ALAN

You sound as though you could be running around like an anxious chicken – looking for greener grass in the next field.
I could tell you - it's all the same - give or take a brass farthing.

PATRICIA

What a quaint expression - what's a brass farthing?
You see! I really ought to know what a brass farthing is.

ALAN

My God - that's really going to change the world!

PATRICIA

It might.
It might be necessary for me to know exactly what a brass farthing is.
The Battle of Waterloo was lost for the want of nail.

ALAN

Really? A brass nail perhaps?

*This following sequence to match the drama of the
narration – aided by an excited Patricia –excited also
by the storm – is intercut and lit by flashes of lightning
and bursts of thunder – the two naked bodies on the
bed. The drama of the storm suits the "battle-drama"
of her tale.*

PATRICIA

Because of an insignificant nail missing from
the shoe of an insignificant horse.

ALAN

Really?

PATRICIA

The horse could not be shoed and the lieutenant
could not ride.

ALAN

Really?

PATRICIA

And deliver his message.

ALAN

Really?

PATRICIA

About the imminent arrival of the Prussians.

ALAN

Really?

PATRICIA

From the hidden left flank.

ALAN

Really?

PATRICIA

No nail – no horse-shoe - no horse – no
delivery of message – Napoleon is taken by
surprise – panic, rout, disaster, defeat,
capitulation – end of the world as they knew it.

ALAN

Really?

PATRICIA

Start of the modern world.

ALAN

Really? The modern world starts with a brass
nail?
Or rather starts with a missing brass nail?

PATRICIA

The start of now.
All for the sake of a missing nail.

ALAN

You wish.
Never that easy.

PATRICIA

Fuck me.

ALAN

That is the invitation I was waiting for.
My prick has been awake and trembling for
half an hour.

*The couple make love. Their bodies lit by the lightning
of the storm through the open windowed-door that
leads on the balcony that looks out over the city. They*

fuck and enjoy it. Alan's hands eagerly search all over her body. The camera sometimes watches the city horizon and the sky lit by grand flashes of lightning – extravagant forks and sheets and green-tinged explosions. They reach orgasm – she first and then him. They part.

APARTMENT BALCONY
Night. Interior with Exterior View. Thunderstorm. Summer.

Standing on the balcony watching the storm and lit by lightning flashes – with lashings of rain – he naked, she wrapped in a sheet from the bed. The conversation is amused and bantering.

ALAN

For a hypothetical virgin – you were not at all bad.

PATRICIA

"You are gracious sir, she said,"

ALAN

Was my comment that condescending?

PATRICIA

It was certainly full of masculine superiority.

ALAN

Ok. Chastised. What about you?

PATRICIA

Well I enjoyed it – it's true – I like the size and shape of your prick – its fits me nicely. Not so sure about your heavy breathing – giving me an impression of Olympic stress - as though you were trying to impress me in some way – break records?
And your two fingers in my arse was unfamiliar – I suppose I could get used to it.

ALAN

Are we likely to repeat this happy meeting?

PATRICIA

We could. I enjoyed it enough I think for a
repeat performance I suppose. Maybe.

ALAN

Too many qualifications?

PATRICIA

I would like to make some suggestions.

ALAN

Go ahead.

PATRICIA

Ever tried shaving?
I like to see a completely naked prick.

ALAN

You could do it for me.

PATRICIA

No. You do it.
And I wait in anticipation to see you very
naked and very vulnerable.

ALAN

You know I could fall in love with you.

PATRICIA

Because I make you shave your prick and make
you feel vulnerable?

ALAN

You are the stuff love could be made from.

PATRICIA

Fuck me.
I thought it was me who was looking for the
love.
You were only supposed to be in it for the sex.

PART 3.

SECTION 11

NIGHT TRAM-RIDE
NIGHT. INTERIOR WITH EXTERIOR VIEW. SUMMER.

Patricia and Alan in the back end of an empty tram late at night.

ALAN
Let me ask you.
Does the sensation of a tram ride, however local, in any way satisfy your desire for travel?

PATRICIA
Hmmm? Official question? Yes, you could say that. Bit unambitious.

ALAN
I wanted to be a tram driver when I was a kid.

PATRICIA
Who didn't?

ALAN
Females are not supposed to want to be tram drivers.

PATRICIA
Discrimination.

ALAN
Supposing I was driving the tram – would you want to be a passenger?

PATRICIA
I'd be scared.

ALAN
Why?

PATRICIA
You probably would not be doing it for the right reasons.

ALAN
Being?

PATRICIA
To get me home and into bed?
With your left hand steering my right breast and your right hand holding my brake.

She puts his hand on her breast.

ALAN
Patricia – you know I have a confession.

PATRICIA
Oh? You must surely have been brought up a Catholic.

ALAN
I don't like that name - Patricia.

PATRICIA
Sorry, it's my identity.

ALAN
Patricia is a male Patrick. It's a substitute name. Sticking breasts on a male saint is not satisfactory.

PATRICIA
Don't worry. Tonight there is nothing male and nothing saintly about me.
And I am the real thing. I am no substitute.

ALAN
Prove it. Let me see your breasts.

PATRICIA
You do know, don't you, that this is a public transport vehicle?

She unbuttons her blouse, manoeuvres the clasp of her brassiere and shows him her breast. He bends forward and kisses and then sucks her nipple.

ALAN
And which part of you is the brake?

PATRICIA
I have always thought it was never the principle of going fast that was at stake, but the confidence to go fast, knowing that you had reliable brakes to stop exactly when you wanted to stop, if you wanted to stop. Having a safe and reliable brake gives you every confidence to go very fast.

ALAN
Are you wanting to stop already?

He sucks her nipple ravenously. Her breast is wet with his saliva.

PATRICIA
On the contrary. I enjoy your driving abilities. You can go faster - if you like. Though going slow is also good. You could make a good tram driver. All those years ago when you were a little boy, could you ever have thought you could drive a tram like this?

ALAN
Can I put my hand on your brake now?

PATRICIA
Of course. In fact, I insist. A good driver always has his brake in mind.

He puts his hand between her legs.

ALAN
Are there cameras on these trams?

PATRICIA
I have yet to see one.

ALAN
Can the driver see us?

He lifts her skirt and puts his hand in her underwear.

PATRICIA
He should have his eye on the road.

ALAN
Do you think we have something useful in the way of a relationship?

PATRICIA
Definitely.

ALAN
I could believe that too.

PATRICIA
I like your prick. It is useful. And it believes in relationships.

He rips her knickers open and gets out his erect penis, lifts her up and enters her vagina. She gasps. They copulate. Not vigorously enough for her.

PATRICIA
Can you drive this tram a little faster?

ALAN
Nobody sober uses a tram after one o'clock in the morning.

PATRICIA
My father sometimes does.

ALAN
Your father?

PATRICIA
Coming home from locking up the church.

ALAN
What would you say if your father got on this tram this very moment?

PATRICIA
Ah! Hello dad – this is Alan, a serial tram driver with the biggest cock, I, for one, have ever known.

Alan pauses.

PATRICIA
Don't worry, he takes a number 15.

They become excited.

ALAN
My God, I have never done this before.

PATRICIA
I should hope not.

ALAN
Patricia, do we have a future?

PATRICIA
If we don't get arrested.

ALAN
Is this a criminal offence?

PATRICIA
I have absolutely no idea.

ALAN
I have a confession.

PATRICIA
Again? Confessions are becoming a habit. And at a time like this?

ALAN
I could get used to you.

PATRICIA
You have sort of said that before.
What exactly do you mean?

ALAN
You enjoy what I like.

PATRICIA
You mean fucking on a tram?

ALAN
It need not necessarily be on a tram.

The tram stops and someone at the front end gets on. Patricia looks over Alan's shoulder. It is an elderly man. He wears a dog collar. He is probably a priest. He sits with his back to them some thirty seats away. Patricia smiles.

PATRICIA
Keep going. Don't stop.

ALAN
I could ride this tram all night.

PATRICIA
Well I have a confession now.

ALAN
What is that?

PATRICIA
My father has just got on this tram.

ALAN
What!?

*The tram stops at lights and an elderly woman standing
on the pavement close to the tram, looks in the window
and sees what they are doing. She watches with
unjudgemental interest. They do not see her. They
consummate.
Patricia opens her eyes and sees the woman and smiles,
and the woman smiles back. And the tram moves on.
They stare at one another. And part – and try discretely
to arrange their clothing.*

ALAN
Well, do you think that was a first?

PATRICIA
Fucking on a tram with a priest on board?
Knowing this city, probably not.

She looks out the window.

PATRICIA
You know we have gone way past my stop?
This is the last tram and I will have to walk
home.

ALAN
You could stay the night with me.

PATRICIA
Is that wise?

ALAN
Why not?

PATRICIA
I might see the way you live and be shocked.

ALAN
I doubt it.
I have another confession.

PATRICIA
Oh God! Another? My father could move in
permanently.
Why does he need a church? A tram will do.

ALAN
I could fall in love with you.

PATRICIA
Is it that bad?

ALAN
Much worse.
I am in love with you.

SECTION 12

ALAN'S APARTMENT BATHROOM
Night. Interior. Summer.

Patricia and Alan both naked in his bath in an untidy bathroom. In the gloomy light centred over the bath, we can see the walls are covered in various forms of calligraphy – cut from newspapers, books, posters and apparently written by Alan himself. A great many of the hand-drawn words look like practice-draughts for street graffiti.
Alan declares love. Patricia makes conditions on their relationship – efficient contraception, no smoking, better diet.

ALAN
This – as you can see - is my bath.
In my bathroom.

PATRICIA
I have noticed.

ALAN
And I am very happy.

PATRICIA
I am pleased for you.

ALAN
And of course I am pleased for myself.
Do you think this could ripen into something really valuable?

PATRICIA
Are you implying it is not valuable now?

ALAN
Patricia, I want it to last.

PATRICIA
Well, I am happy that it has gone this far it is true.
And I admit to being surprised.
But …

ALAN
But what?

PATRICIA
I am not feeling in love.

ALAN
Oh!?
I am.

PATRICIA
You are?
What does it feel like?

ALAN
Painful.

PATRICIA
Oh? Why? What suddenly happened to your self-confessed happiness?

ALAN
I have a terrible feeling that I am going to lose you.

PATRICIA
That's pessimistic. I am not planning to go anywhere. Yet.

ALAN
You see?
When you have something that is valuable to you - it brings you up short.

You find yourself catching your breath, or your
breath you find is catching you up.
Recently I have become unaccustomly
breathless.

PATRICIA

Well you know I think that I am not not
enjoying myself.
But if we continue like this - I do have some
conditions

ALAN

Oh?

PATRICIA

Unconditional love - I think - I know - I have
read - I have been told – what do I know?
… is not at all necessarily entirely desirable.

ALAN

That is a great deal of qualification.

PATRICIA

Well I am hesitant for both of us.
For me hesitant because you must know I am
insecure.
I was looking for one thing with extras and I
found something else.
And for you because I am not so sure you have
the capacity to agree to my conditions.

ALAN

Try me.

PATRICIA

Contraceptives.

ALAN

Oh?

PATRICIA

Why oh?

ALAN

I thought you wanted a baby.

PATRICIA

That was in the original plan but - I think and I
know you understand me when I say we are not
exactly working to the original plan.
No smoking.

ALAN

Oh?

PATRICIA

Why Oh?

ALAN

Oh - I can give up.

PATRICIA

Wear underpants.

ALAN

Oh? Don't you find it sexy to not to?

PATRICIA

Maybe – but it's more hygienic.
Better diet.

ALAN

For me or you?

PATRICIA

For you.

ALAN

No more supermarket take-away dinners?
Are you going to cook?

PATRICIA

That's a sloppy answer.
Alan – I am going to try not to accept you at
your worst.

SWIMMING-POOL
DAY. INTERIOR. LUNCHTIME. SUMMER.

*Alan and Patricia are at the swimming-pool where Alan
gives lessons to adults and children. The swimming-
pool is empty of people. Alan, in his swimming-trunks
which demonstrate he has an erection, is in the pool at
the shallow end, Patricia, fully dressed, sits on the
pool-side, her bare feet in the water. Alan becomes
unattractively demanding. Patricia backs off.*

ALAN

I am jealous of all your previous lovers.

PATRICIA

I shouldn't be. There weren't so many.
And they weren't so very good,
And none of them stayed very long.

ALAN

Unbelievable.
I am jealous of everyone who ever kissed you -
or touched you.

PATRICIA

Would that include my grandmother?

ALAN

Who was your first love?
With whom did you lose your virginity?

*Alan manoeuvres Patricia's naked foot in the water to
stoke his erect penis inside his swimming trunks. She
complies but is irritated.*

PATRICIA

Those two things are not down to the same
person.
I never traditionally had the first and the second
can only happen once.
And is it important enough for me to ask you
the same question?

ALAN

It's different for a man.

PATRICIA

Hey ho, here we go.
Why is it different for a man?
Who first discovered the delights of your
prick?

ALAN

My cousin - under my grandmother's table in
the kitchen.
Shall I get it out for you?

PATRICIA

No. It's in evidence enough.

ALAN

I was twelve and I was cuffed around the head
for the pleasure of sticky fingers and an ugly
wailing cousin because I had mussed up her
hair.
Now you.

PATRICIA

Much the same.
Disaster and disappointment leading to guilt
and a long pause
before I could let it happen again.
It was a long time ago.

ALAN

Tell me.

PATRICIA

A boy with Vaseline in his ears, and fumbling
cold hands.
His name was Jack and he called me Jill, which
everyone knew was my second name, and he
wrote a school essay of how he had fucked a
girl in a nursery rhyme, and it was read out in
class and he got an A minus.
I stuck a sharpened pencil in his face, which
sort of proved to the class that he was telling
some sort of truth, but I have the satisfaction of
knowing he has the scar in his cheek to this
day. He is a tram driver on route 21 that takes
you from the cemetery to the asylum.

ALAN

Shall I find him and throw him in a canal?

PATRICIA

He can't or couldn't swim.
And retrospective jealousy is going to be a
waste of time.
And it would be bad for your reputation as a
swimming instructor.
Now stop showing off in those swimming
trunks and buy me lunch.

ALAN

Not till you swim naked with me in the diving-
pool.
It's always completely empty at lunch time.
And the water is deep.
I want the chlorinated water to swirl snakily
around your private parts, between your legs, to
caress your arse and kiss your cunt.

PATRICIA
No!
I am hungry and I am starting to wonder why
you keep wanting to do it in public. What are
you trying to prove? That you can fuck me in
public?

ALAN
No. There will be no one there. And what are
we trying to hide?

PATRICIA
Nothing as seems obvious.

He lunges and pulls her into the water.
PATRICIA
That was very stupid.
I am now soaked and I have to go to work this
afternoon.

He tries to pull her under.
She is swift, avoids his grappling and smashes him
seriously around the head that startles and stings him.
ALAN
That is no way to treat a man who loves you.

She adroitly lifts herself out of the water.

PATRICIA
Alan – you are in love with yourself being in
love.
ALAN
Patricia!
PATRICIA
You are a prick.
And by no means as beautiful as the one
between your legs.

ALAN
Patricia!

PATRICIA
I am an excuse for some mighty arrogant
narcissism on your part.
If you say you love me - wise up.
And try and understand what that really means!

Drenched and dripping water, she leaves.

PART 4

SECTION 14

CINEMA. PATRICIA MEETS MICHAEL
Night. Interior. Summer.

Patricia and Michael, with two cinema seats between them, are watching a film (it could be Manhattan – Woody Allen's film about Manhattan architecture.) in an almost empty cinema - (the Tuschinski Cinema, Amsterdam) - their faces illuminated by the kick-back black and white light from the film. Patricia is weeping whilst watching the film. Michael leans over and passes her a handkerchief. He whispers.

MICHAEL
Hey – seems to me you could use this?

PATRICIA
Thank you.

They both continue to watch in silence.

MICHAEL
Suspension of disbelief hey?

PATRICIA
Shhhh! I am believing.

MICHAEL
Sorry.

They watch in silence.

PATRICIA
Your handkerchief – smells of …

MICHAEL
Parcomyothetilene?

PATRICIA
Is that a drug to make me sleepy prior to rape?

MICHAEL
Wow! You make my handkerchief sound dangerous.
Still - I suppose cinema can be very suggestive - and indeed for some - a drug.
Parcomyothetilene is an anti-perspirent built into washing-powder.
I have only recently learnt how to pronounce it.
My cleaning lady is a laundry-freak.

PATRICIA
Well that's very good to know.

MICHAEL
She would think so.

They watch in silence – Patricia still with tear-stained face.

MICHAEL
But - explain – you are crying – and this is meant to be a comedy.

PATRICIA
I don't hear the audience laughing.

MICHAEL
Not much audience here.

PATRICIA
Just the two of us.

MICHAEL
Could be someone over there.
Though it could be a tailor's dummy.

PATRICIA
Or an abandoned coat and hat.

MICHAEL
Maybe a corpse left over from last night?

She smiles. He moves a seat closer. There is still one empty seat between them.

MICHAEL
Last night they showed a thriller.
And an unimportant corpse fell out of the film?
They will be around eventually to collect it.
Take it back to the property department.
They probably need it in another film.
Just change the hat and they can put it in a costume drama.

PATRICIA
Something like that.

MICHAEL
The usherette put me here to be in company.
We cinema-goers have to stick together in the dark.
Besides I would rather laugh at home – wouldn't you?
Cry at a comedy in the cinema - laugh at a tragedy at home?
That way you don't have to give yourself away to strangers who might think you perverse?

PATRICIA
Something like that.

MICHAEL
Could that be why you are crying?

PATRICIA
Could be.

MICHAEL
This city has the lowest cinema attendance in the world.

PATRICIA
Save Finisterre.

MICHAEL
Finisterre?

PATRICIA
Island in the Atlantic – no cinemas.

MICHAEL
That explains it.

PATRICIA
Family joke.

MICHAEL
Whose family?

PATRICIA
Mine.

MICHAEL
Could never be mine. Nobody in my family ever made jokes.
That's why I have no sense of humour.
I was never taught when to laugh at life's banalities.

PATRICIA
My father's favourite radio programme was the BBC weather forecast.
Finisterre is a bleak rock in the Atlantic surrounded by a thousand square miles of empty sea. And endless storms.
Finisterre - the end of land - in our family

represented the very ultimate in negativity.
Total bleakness. Emptiness. You can't go any
further.
Forever storms at the end of the world.
Viking, Cromarty, Forth, Tyne, Dogger, Fisher,
German Bight, Humber, Thames, Dover,
Wight, Portland, Biscay, Trafalgar, Finisterre.

MICHAEL
Some sort of beautiful dreadful-weather
poetry?
It rains a lot here.
You know that the average Dutch citizen only
goes to the cinema once every two years.

PATRICIA
To get out of the rain?
What are we doing here then?

MICHAEL
I am not an average Dutch citizen. Are you an
average Dutch citizen?

PATRICIA
Yes, I am. You can see how tall I am.
I am obviously living up to Dutch averages.

MICHAEL
What's the average height for a female in this city?

PATRICIA
Around one metre, sixty-eight. Why?

MICHAEL
They say the Dutch are getting taller all the
time,
It's on account of spending so much time in the
dark.

PATRICIA
Well it's not through spending great amounts of
time in the dark of cinemas.

MICHAEL
My mother used to say you grew quicker in the
dark.

PATRICIA
At this rate we will never reach the ceiling.

MICHAEL
And just look at that ceiling.

*They look up at the decorated ceiling dimly lit from the
screen.*

PATRICIA
If I didn't go to the cinema, the audience
average would be worse – much worse.

MICHAEL
Coming alone of course doesn't help.

PATRICIA
My lover doesn't like the cinema.
I have to go on his behalf to make the average
look a little more respectable.

MICHAEL
What is it exactly your lover doesn't like about
the cinema?

PATRICIA
Sharing your emotions in the dark with
strangers like you?

They both laugh.

PATRICIA
Are we sharing emotions?

MICHAEL
Well - we are certainly in the dark

They laugh again - someone says sssshhh. They both look round.

MICHAEL
Good lord! There really is someone else here.

Patricia gets into the seat next to him. She whispers.

PATRICIA
What about your lover?

MICHAEL
If I had one, I could tell you.
I'll arrange to take a lover and come back and tell you.
I am here for the architecture.

PATRICIA
In the dark?

MICHAEL
On the screen and on the ceiling.
This is a movie about architecture.

PATRICIA
Really? I hadn't noticed.

MICHAEL
Well then look at the ceiling.

PATRICIA
Again can't see much.

MICHAEL
You would be surprised - a great deal of architecture looks best at night.
When I walk you home in a minute I could show you what I mean.

PATRICIA
Walk me home? I am not much of a walker.
I am a slave to my tram card.

MICHAEL
Tram routes are not the best architectural routes I am afraid.

SECTION 15

SUBURBAN STREETS
Night. Exterior. Approaching Thunderstorm. Summer.

Michael and Patricia are walking in the suburbs at one in the morning - looking at 1920s Amsterdam School architecture by street-lights. There are distant rumbles of thunder.

MICHAEL

Look at that – elaborate brickwork for an end wall facing away from the road – the bricks are laid small side out, Flemish bond, built around a pre-formed wooden former, probably designed by Erik van Coving, who could always be guaranteed to raise the standard of a blank wall-space.

PATRICIA

It looks as though it might rain
Did I hear thunder?

MICHAEL

Architecture in the rain.
We will be able to see why the roofs are so interesting.
Excessive slope to anticipate swift run-off.
Get the water to the ground as quickly as possible.
Flat roofs are very unusual in this city.
All the Amsterdam School architects were rain specialists.
Look at that coping – the way it joins the roof-line - probably influenced by Macintosh.
Charles Rennie Macintosh.

PATRICIA

Raincoat?

MICHAEL

Indeed. His middle name "Rennie" is almost a diminutive for "raincoat".

PATRICIA

Sounds as though he could be the ideal Dutch architect.

MICHAEL

Scottish. Glasgow.
Died of cancer of the tongue – too much sucking on his pipe.

PATRICIA

Or like you - too much talking?

MICHAEL

Sorry.

PATRICIA

Are you an architect?

MICHAEL

No. Entertainments accountant.

PATRICIA

Architecture and accountancy? Do they mix?

MICHAEL

Not so often.
Even entertainment and accounting don't mix that well.

They laugh. They are enjoying themselves very much in one another's company.

PATRICIA

Hey. I am far from home and need to pee.

MICHAEL

Oh? How can I help?

Do it for you?

My office is not so far away.

PATRICIA

How far?

MICHAEL

Twenty minutes' brisk walk.

PATRICIA

Can't wait that long. And brisk walking will make it more urgent.

MICHAEL

Go and do it on the grass.

There's nobody about.

PATRICIA

You're about.

MICHAEL

Hell - I won't look.

And I am only interested in the architecture.

PATRICIA

Somehow your "only" sounds disparaging.

MICHAEL

Hey - sorry.

PATRICIA

Can you rewind that "only" and show me you are sorry.

MICHAEL

Hell! "I am only interested in the architecture."

I see what you mean – sorry – disparagement

not at all intended.

My only excuse was to assist your modesty.

PATRICIA

A real gentleman.

She crouches to urinate. They are separated by a low hedge in a Dutch garden.

MICHAEL

You are peeing in a typical Dutch garden. Not much cover, I'm afraid.

Low cut box hedges, white gravel - now if you were peeing in an English garden, there is so much cover I would loose you.

PATRICIA

National preferences – deliberate immodesty, excessive modesty.

Display and Hide. Reveal and conceal.

MICHAEL

Perhaps more complicated than that.

The Dutch don't want to suggest they have anything to hide in the first place.

Very Calvinist.

Have you got anything to hide?

Hiding things stimulates envy.

The English are convinced women don't pee anyway.

English women lose waste fluids by evaporation.

PATRICIA

The air over England is full of clouds of evaporated female urine?

MICHAEL

And we now are also being very Dutch -
excessive dispassionate discussion of scatology.
Don't concern yourself. Dutch gardens were
not necessarily made to pee in.
But the extra nitrogen and ammonia helps -
nutritional.

PATRICIA

I will remember that.

MICHAEL

It is an obvious fact but strange when you
repeat it.
That all the human urine you smell in city
streets is male.
Women rarely pee in the street.

PATRICIA

At least not in this district.

*Patricia has finished and is standing up, pulling up her
knickers, now oblivious to her modesty in front of
Michael. The crashes of thunder are closer.*

MICHAEL

Do you want to borrow my handkerchief
again?

PATRICIA

How thoughtful of you.

MICHAEL

Not so many men are prepared to realise peeing
for a woman can be a moist business.

PATRICIA

Strange comment.

MICHAEL

Strictly from a male point of view of course.
And, am I allowed to say this … ?

PATRICIA

Go on – try.

MICHAEL

I must say I would quite like the smell of your
urine on my handkerchief.

PATRICIA

Well – that could be the strangest come-on I
have ever heard.
Hey! Here comes the rain.

MICHAEL

Quick! Let's see if we can steal a bike
Don't worry I'll put it back tomorrow.

*In the pouring rain, they steal a bike to cycle to his
office.*

SECTION 16

BIKE RIDE IN THE RAIN
NIGHT. EXTERIOR. THUNDERSTORM. SUMMER.

*Patricia sits on the back of the bike ridden by Michael.
Shouted conversation on the bike in rain-swept street lit
by lightning and rumbled by thunder.*

MICHAEL
This city was built of wood and frequently on
fire.
The smell of wood-ash never lifted.
Then they started to build in brick.
Then Benjamin Franklin invented the lightning
conductor and now we are all safe. Safe as
houses in fact.

PATRICIA
Strange phrase.

MICHAEL
Compensates for when we were not as "safe as
houses".
Fire insurance was invented in this city.
Which is a surprise considering all the water in
the canals.
Householders could easily be their own
firemen.
A bike is a sort of lightning conductor.

PATRICIA
Jesus! Shall I get off?
Don't the rubber tyres help?

MICHAEL
A flash of one million kilowatts is not going to
respect four centimetres of rubber tyre.

PATRICIA
I really do think I better get off.

MICHAEL
You can. We are here.

PART 5

MICHAEL'S OFFICE
NIGHT. INTERIOR. THUNDERSTORM. SUMMER.

Arrival at Michael's office. Full of toy Noah's Arks.
Evidence of small children.
They drip water on the floor. Michael switches on lights
and plugs in a kettle.

PATRICIA
Jesus - I am soaked.

MICHAEL
There is a bathroom and a shower.
My business partner has a flat upstairs.
I am sure we can find more towels.
Maybe even a drying machine of some sort.
I will make some coffee and toast.

PATRICIA
These Noah's Arks - are they a flood warning?

MICHAEL
Paul is obsessed with the prospect of animals
drowning.

Thunder. Michael plugs in the toaster which overloads
a weak system which fuses and the lights go out.

MICHAEL
God! Overloaded again!

PATRICIA
Lights, coffee-machine, dryer, toaster – doesn't
take much - he should get it fixed.

MICHAEL
He should. I should. There is a torch here
somewhere and maybe some candles.

Thunder crash. He lights candles.
Patricia starts to strip off her wet clothing. Michael
pours the cold water from the defunct kettle into two
glasses and sets them on the table.

PATRICIA
Getting off wet clothes is like getting out of
your own skin.

MICHAEL
Let me help.

PATRICIA
I get over-excited by thunder.

MICHAEL
So did my grandmother. She was very
superstitious.
With a storm coming - she would wrap all the
knives and forks in green baize like you get on
billiard tables.
She thought electricity was red and hard – the
soft green baize would absorb it.
She hid the milk – sure it would curdle.
Pulled out all the plugs – though her house was
only fitted with electricity after much resistance
- she was used to gas – she was utterly
convinced electricity was like gas and would
leak out of the wall-plugs.

Patricia is soon standing, candle-lit in just her knickers,
drying her hair in a white towel.

PATRICIA
I would have liked to have met your
grandmother.

Michael is talking on and on – getting excited by seeing Patricia's almost naked body. Patricia realises his excitement and is playfully smiling. She drinks water from a glass.

MICHAEL

And you had to stay away from chimneys and fireplaces because lighting was devious and would come down the chimney to get you. I was the eldest grandchild and she reckoned eldest children in a family of boys were more likely to be struck by lightning then their brothers – so she protected me most. I had to crawl under the table, or if there wasn't a table, hide under her skirts and when I got too old to hide under her skirt, she covered my head with her apron.

Michael takes all his clothes off, wraps a towel around his waist.

PATRICIA

Can you cover my head with your apron? Do you have an apron?

MICHAEL

I would rather hide under your skirts.

PATRICIA

Why not?

Michael takes the towel from around his waist and covers Patricia's head with it as she sits on a low desk. He dries her hair. His genitals are close to her face.

PATRICIA

(she whispers) Hey! You smell good.

MICHAEL

I thought you had a lover.

PATRICIA

I do. But you still smell good.
My lover says he loves me and I sort of believe him.
I know that I don't love him.
I wish I did. I really do wish I did.
But I know it isn't on.
It would be good if I loved him, but I don't.

MICHAEL

You have said that three times.

PATRICIA

Maybe that is what I was crying about in the cinema.
I was anxiously looking for love and he wasn't.
He was anxiously looking for sex.
But he found the love and I found the sex that went with it.
It was all the wrong way round.

MICHAEL

Sex can be a great consolation for missing love.

PATRICIA

I know. I know. I know.
I certainly enjoy the sex and I can indeed rhapsodize endlessly over his beautiful prick - a pale white cannon resting on summer plums.

MICHAEL

Hey! That's some poetical excitement of a prick!

PATRICIA

Can you fall in love with a prick and not its owner?

MICHAEL
With or without his consent?

PATRICIA
You see I am looking hard for love.
Maybe I am looking too hard.
Maybe you could teach me how not to look too
hard so that I might find it?
You are good at architecture, rich in anecdote,
poor with electricity, but good with storms –
and obviously had a very loving grandmother.
Why don't I practice on you what my lover had
practiced on me?
Kiss me.

They kiss.

PATRICIA
Now show me what you can do for me.
You have bored me all evening with
Amsterdam's architecture lit by lightning.
Now show me your architecture lit by
lightning.

MICHAEL
I am not so sure that I can show you - what was
it – "a white cannon lying on autumn plums"?

*She switches on a torch and shines it at Michael's
genitals, flicking it on and off to simulate lightning.*

PATRICIA
Nothing very military or autumnal about you.
But very upstanding and summery I think.
Very architectural I suppose.
Neat but nicely bold. Chubby I'd say.
A nice chubby prick.
Somehow it reminds me of rabbits.

A chubby stump of a thick prick reminding me
of rabbits

MICHAEL
Rabbits? Really?

PATRICIA
Endearing I'd say.
It wouldn't scare anyone.
I like it. I really like it.
It really suits you.
I'd quite like to host your rabbit in my burrow.
Would you like to fuck me?

MICHAEL
I would like that very much.
But you know what they say about rabbits?

*She turns away from him and she takes off her knickers.
He sees her buttocks.*

PATRICIA
They proliferate very easily?
There is an electric storm going on.
So much electricity in the air could act like a
deterrent, I suppose.

MICHAEL
Or an aphrodisiac?

PATRICIA
Let's take a risk.
Which way would you like to fuck me?

MICHAEL
You are offering me your backside?
Rabbits do it from the backside.
I'll take the offer.

*He holds her from behind, kissing her neck, rubbing his
face in her damp hair. He slides his hands around her
shoulders and down to her breasts. She turns around in
his arms and they kiss mouth to mouth. She holds his
hips and reaches for his buttocks. He bends to kiss her
nipples and reaches to stroke her belly and places his
hand between her legs. She holds his prick. He turns
her around. She bends over the desk and he enters her
vaginally from behind as the thunder rumbles and the
lightning illuminates them in the darkness, the torch
shining a straight beam at Patricia's face and the three
candles adding steady warm flickering light.*
*The lightning illuminates the wooden animals of the
late 19th century Noah's Ark laid out on the desktop.
He copulates silently. She quietly moans at each stroke.
She moves her head from side to side. He feels for her
breasts and massages her shoulders and backbone and
massages her hips. As he nears orgasm he gets slower
and slower and quietly, rhythmically grunts. She is now
silent, concentrating. Finally, he is still. For a moment
it seems he has reached orgasm. Then he shouts and
comes. He has jerked the table and a glass of water
spills over the animals of the Noah's Ark, "drowning"
them.*

PATRICIA

There you are. You have spilt the water and all
the animals have drowned.
That's not at all what happened in the Flood.
I suggest you read your Bible.

MICHAEL

God. Paul will be distraught. All those dead
giraffes!

They kiss deeply.

PART 6

SECTION 18

THE BEACH AT NIGHT
NIGHT. EXTERIOR. SUMMER.

Looking towards the beach from the sea - naked love-making between Patricia and Michael in the sea, under the moon, up to their armpits in the water. They hug and kiss, hold hands, turn about, clasp one another, rub noses, strongly embrace, happily banter. Patricia is especially happy. The lights of the city shine on the far horizon.

PATRICIA
I used to make lists.
Things to achieve.
To get my grammar right.
Dutch grammar is especially difficult.
Learn the right vocabulary so I could talk properly about philosophy, psychology, cooking …

MICHAEL
… architecture?

PATRICIA
And architecture. Yes, architecture.
Ride a horse,
Fire a pistol,
Run a marathon,
Dance the tango with the right sort of strained grimace on my face.

MICHAEL
Merely New Year resolutions. They don't really get you very far.

PATRICIA
I think the best way to go about it at my age - since I am certainly not going back to school, Is to learn to be very satisfactorily independent and entirely self-supportive.
With pleasure and joy - not like some ghastly chore.
And to satisfy every curiosity as soon as possible – no delays.
So - travel has to be the first priority.
I only know one city - this city - in the world well - very well - very well enough to be a tour guide to the specialist.

They look at the lights of the city on the horizon

MICHAEL
Specialist what?

PATRICIA
Speleologist, water mechanic, laptop dancer, dog fanatic.

MICHAEL
Didn't know we had caves under our feet?

PATRICIA
I only know one country in the world.
I can read and count.
I am personable.
I can command good small talk and thanks to a reasonable education I can speak two languages well and another one not so badly.
Equipped - you see - well enough to travel.

MICHAEL
Money?

PATRICIA
Yes - there's a problem.
I have enough to keep me going - economy
class - for a year I reckon.
And then we'll have to see.
I want to use everything I have.

MICHAEL
Sounds promising.
Cunt and arse, appendix and back-teeth?

PATRICIA
Yes - if necessary - those as well.
Earwax, navel-fluff and how to pronounce
shibboleth.

MICHAEL
You said it - 90 percent of sex is recreational.

PATRICIA
What's recreationally sexy about shibboleth?
I don't want to go on treading water.
I want to do some really serious walking
around the world.

MICHAEL
Get a pair of good shoes.

PATRICIA
What do I know?
I probably eat the same twenty meals over and
over again.

MICHAEL
Eight types of meat.

PATRICIA
Twenty types of vegetable.

MICHAEL
Twenty types of fruit.

PATRICIA
Not good enough. Simply not good enough.

*Crying seagulls fly overhead. They both look up into
the dark sky. No birds to be seen.*

PATRICIA
There must be over ten thousand bird species –
I've only ever seen maybe a couple of hundred.
And the only bird I have ever eaten is chicken
shacked up in a battery farm.

MICHAEL
Your bird-eating plan sound exploitative.

PATRICIA
Don't take me so literally.
You know what I mean.
Michael - there's lot to eat in the world.

MICHAEL
And many ways to starve.

PATRICIA
I have the wherewithal for another twelve
months not to starve.
I must make the most of it.

MICHAEL
How about drink?

PATRICIA
I don't drink that much.
What do I drink?

Tea and coffee. I don't like beer.
 I drink wine, vodka, cognac.
I like port.
Pretty limited.

MICHAEL
How about water - seawater?

*He makes to dunk her head in the water. They splash
and fool about and then upend dive - showing their
backsides mooning in the moonlight. Then they walk
naked out of the sea and make love on the sand. We
hear them from a distance*

PATRICIA
Watch out! Don't get sand in my cunt!

MICHAEL
First then you have to lick it off my prick.

PATRICIA
That's easy - it's so little.

MICHAEL
It's the cold water.

PATRICIA
…. and salty.

MICHAEL
To make it tasty.

We leave them giggling on the beach

IN MICHAEL'S APARTMENT
Night. Interior. Summer.

*Scene to show Patricia's developing love. Night-time -
sitting in the dark. They are both naked. She sitting on a
table. He sitting on a chair, between her knees. He
paints her mouth with a high-gloss lipstick.*

PATRICIA
Do you believe in love?

MICHAEL
As an idea, as a strategy, I believe in it.
Keep your head still.
It is a method we have devised to help us
negotiate a large difficulty.
Love is a man-made thing – or if you like - a
woman-made thing - to explain and justify us
getting together to fuck.

PATRICIA
My parents loved each other, but I am pretty
certain they didn't fuck more than fifty times in
their entire lives.
And they lived long lives.
If my father had made all the decisions it would
have been even less.

MICHAEL
Although I cannot help but say that is a sad
pity, and a waste of bodies - fifty times is
probably enough.
Enough times certainly to make you.
Show me.

She pouts to demonstrate the lipstick.

MICHAEL

I can only believe that procreation can be the excuse for living.
We live to procreate.

PATRICIA

...... and we procreate to live?

He begins to paint her nipples with the high-gloss lipstick

MICHAEL

I believe it is a one-way trip only.
A good Darwinian believes that there is an evolutionary reason for every goddamed thing.
I cannot for the life of me think of any other excuse for living other than to procreate.

PATRICIA

That might sound like we are all putting off making some almighty decision about something.
Passing the buck. Leaving it all for the next in line to undertake.
But I asked you "Do you believe in love?" I did not ask you for Darwin's opinion.

MICHAEL

I agree with Darwin. I believe in love as a strategy to procreate.
Love makes a healthy little protective cocoon.
(looking at her lip-sticked nipples)
Beautiful.

PATRICIA

But sticky.

MICHAEL

First of all, and certainly in the modern world where we all supposed to be civilised and considerate – it gives us permission to fuck.
Open your legs.
Did you know lipstick originated with a desire to directly arouse the male interest by making the vaginal lips very red and very noticeable?

PATRICIA

Like baboons?
I am certain - Mister Animal-Man – that it was exactly the other way around.

MICHAEL

Love - once upon a time gave us permission and excuse to get married and then fuck.
Marriage has dropped out of the equation.
And then, entirely beyond our control, out of our hands, chances are - the sperm sets to work on the egg - and we are off – nothing to do with us at all anymore.
Only thing we have to do is stay alive.

PATRICIA

Rape creates the same result.

MICHAEL

You are absolutely correct.
But love continues to help to create an environment that the pregnant mother survives in happily enough and then presents an environment for the child to flourish and be nourished and grow and then –

PATRICIA

What then?

MICHAEL

Well - the seven-year itch could kick in?
Seeing the woman and the child flourishing, the

man moves off to try to start the whole thing up again some other place.

Michael admires Patricia's lip-sticked vagina.

MICHAEL
There look at that. You are now five times as desirable.

PATRICIA
And five times as sticky. You sure it's wise to put lipstick on my cunt?

MICHAEL
Tested on animals.

PATRICIA
You mean baboons? Thank you very much.

MICHAEL
 And they didn't die.

PATRICIA
How do you know?

MICHAEL
I don't - but I do know that the male animal does his utmost to reproduce himself as many times as he can. And he'll try anything. Driven by the almost unfightable mechanics of lust and an inbuilt drive to replicate himself. With as many different women as he can to spread his genetic material.

PATRICIA
You mean like a hippo spreading his shit with his tail?

SECTION 20

A FIELD
DAY. EXTERIOR. SUNNY DAY. SUMMER.

Michael has driven his car into a meadow of long grass and they are lying naked in the grass making love. Flesh and grass and grass stems and wild flowers, he on top of her. Details of buttocks and flowers, her breasts and his chest and nipples. Insects. They finish their copulation and lay back - legs spread - he with a moist prick, she with damp pubic hair.

PATRICIA
Michael, in times like these I am going to be honest.

MICHAEL
Oh "in times like these"?
Sounds history making. I think we might need some music.
I could turn on the car radio? Shall I do that?

PATRICIA
If you must.

He does. Naked, he walks to the car. She watches him. He turns on the radio, fiddles with the dials. Buoyant Handel classical music turns up – the stuff to warm and rejoice the heart. He returns to Patricia and lies down in the grass again, his head on her belly.

PATRICIA
"In times like these" - apparently a woman is supposed to feint and hide and bluff.
But if I am going to be a professional human being I have to be honest and suffer the consequences.

MICHAEL
What are you planning?
It sounds almost ominous? And life
threatening.

PATRICIA
I am planning to tell you that I love you.

MICHAEL
Oh?

PATRICIA
That is an adequate response?

MICHAEL
Are you sure after all we've been discussing -
both of us believe in love?

PATRICIA
I do.

MICHAEL
Oh! How do you do?

PATRICIA
Well - first characteristic - the attraction I have
for you will not go away.
I think almost constantly about you.
Why is that?
Because the signs - on the face of it - are not
good.

MICHAEL
Oh?

PATRICIA
You are overweight.
You have a boring job.
And although I love the little thing dearly - you
have a smallish prick.

You seem not at all to be ambitious.
You wear glasses.
I doubt whether you will ever have any money.
Ever.
It could be that I think you are in fact - lazy.
I was planning to fall in love according to the
rules,
And I find that the rulebook is indeed correct.
The object of desire in fact - as they repeatedly
say - is almost curiously irrelevant.

MICHAEL
Thank you for all these delightful compliments.

PATRICIA
Michael – since I so badly want to fall in love.
Am I tricking myself with you?
Am I being deceived?
Is my heart deceiving me?
First it was just damp eyes at bedtime.
Now sometimes in the middle of the afternoon
– hopelessly after a morning and before an
evening – that blank empty space of the day - I
weep buckets for you Michael.
And then - sitting on my sofa in the evenings -
at that sad hour - the magic hour they call it –
some magic! – I spend dreaming endlessly
about you.
Love is not pleasant – often all I remember so
far is some pain.
Rocking myself on the bed with stomach ache.
Not going to work - getting drunk at lunch-time
- staring at the walls.

MICHAEL
Oh?

PATRICIA
Please stop saying oh?

MICHAEL
I am sorry. But I agree - it is not a very useful response.

PATRICIA
So you don't love me?

MICHAEL
Jesus Patricia! I have tried to explain.
Though - probably you are right - as much to myself as to you - what it's all about.

PATRICIA
Michael, how come at gone thirty-three you have no children?
With all this stuff you promote about procreation?

MICHAEL
I cannot eradicate the programming but I don't necessarily want the end product.

PATRICIA
How the Hell am I going to use all this?

MICHAEL
Up to you I am thinking.

PATRICIA
It's a cheat.
Evolutionary mechanisms are cheating on us.

MICHAEL
No they are not.
But I don't think they care either way.
Why should they?
Our satisfaction is a by-product - if you are lucky - a bonus.

PATRICIA
Evolution is just a cuckoo selfishly out for itself.

MICHAEL
Absolutely.
Despite all our wayward pressures and persuasions - it is keeping us in line.
Every strategy for evolution wins.
Even in a sense if it fails, it wins.
If it fails it was never meant to win.
I love to fuck.
It is the most delightful physical experience ever.
But don't get any funny ideas.
Don't bring in anything else – God, mysticism, spiritual well-being.
There have been years and years and years of fixing evolution by repeated mutation to make fucking as exciting and enjoyable as it can be.
Pressures, anatomies, liquids, smells, temperatures, softness, hardnesses, the right amount of dangerous pleasure to the right amounts of sweet pain.
And it has paid off – absolutely - apparently more successful in the human species than in any other species.
I always always love fucking. So does every human male on the planet.
The desire never fails.
After all – there are thirty-five billion of us.
Just right to match thirty-five billion females.

PATRICIA
Evolution wasn't so very kind to you.

MICHAEL
How so?

PATRICIA

Surely to match your desire it should have
given you a bigger cock?

MICHAEL

The size and the desire are not so necessarily
related.
And it does not seem to matter to you.
Can I be blunt?

PATRICIA

You just have been.

MICHAEL

You have told me you love me – bingo!
Which means I am to be encouraged to fuck you,
And certainly enjoy myself – evolution wins
out of that enjoyment.

PATRICIA

I don't.

MICHAEL

Yes, you do.
Your delightful body is designed to make
babies.
Despite what might be going on in your head,
Your body has declared its purposes.

PATRICIA

How about what is going on in my heart?

MICHAEL

Patricia - come on - nothing is going on in your
heart.
Except a mechanism to pump blood around
your body.
Whatever it is - it is going on in your head not
your heart.

All this talk is even a mechanism of evolution.
Just to talk about it is to encourage it.
Shall we do it again?

SECTION 21

ON THE BEACH
DAY. EXTERIOR. SUNNY DAY. SUMMER.

*A game of bat and ball on the beach. They play
barefoot in the sand - whilst talking – their
conversation broken into small snatches of dialogue.
The camera often watching them in close-up.*

PATRICIA

… and looking - I want to do some looking -
real looking.
Not pictures-in-books stuff – though you could
spend a lifetime doing that and I might.
But the real things – white Siberian tigers.

MICHAEL

Unlikely. Patricia – please concentrate.

PATRICIA

Twins. I want to meet twins.

MICHAEL

Pardon?

PATRICIA

Mountains - and not from a plane.
Motorbikes, tattoos.
Should I get a tattoo between anus and vagina?

MICHAEL

Can I be the first to see?

PATRICIA

Now you're losing concentration.

MICHAEL

I am thinking of the writing on your body.

PATRICIA

Architecture.
Buildings.
Steps and stairs.
I have always been interested in steps and
stairs.

MICHAEL

Weird lady.

PATRICIA

Weird ladies!
Witches, female prime-ministers, giraffe-
necked women.

MICHAEL

Don't exist anymore.
Why don't you use the other side of the bat?

PATRICIA

Flea circuses.

MICHAEL

Never existed.

PATRICIA

Live octopus - not in an Italian restaurant.

MICHAEL

Easy. Visit a zoo. Go scuba diving - take a
package holiday.
Don't hit so hard.

PATRICIA

No packages anything.

MICHAEL

You going alone?

PATRICIA

I think I have to.
Because I don't think you'll be coming with
me?

MICHAEL

Then you're going to be lonely.

PATRICIA

Probably on and off - but aren't we all?
Cheap hotels. And smart hotels.

MICHAEL

Patricia I am spending my energy jumping for
impossible hits.

PATRICIA

I want to sleep in a different bed every night of
the year.
365 beds.

MICHAEL

Tiresome – all that packing and unpacking.
I could come with you as far as Istanbul.
I am not so interested in leaving Europe.

PATRICIA

How provincial.

MICHAEL

Not necessarily.
As I have said, there are some seven billion in
the world.
And ten per cent of those are in Europe.
If I travel outside Europe, I'd be the provincial
because I know nothing about "outside Europe".

Europe's enough.
How long you going to keep this up?

PATRICIA

What the travelling?

MICHAEL

No - the hitting too hard so I am a jumping
circus.
And isn't it all superficial?
Patricia - you are just a restless tourist.

PATRICIA

In love.
I am a restless tourist in love.
With you.
Goddam it!

She hits the ball very hard into the sea.

PART 7

SECTION 22

BEACH CAFÉ
DAY. EXTERIOR. SUNNY. SUMMER.

Patricia and Michael are sitting in the sun in a beach café terrace on the edge of the dunes, facing the beach and the sea, drinking coffee. Some way behind them is a largish ugly hotel. Patricia has her shoes off.

PATRICIA
I am buying a new suitcase.
And keeping it ready at the top of the stairs.
To remind me that I need to travel.

MICHAEL
I keep my suitcases in the downstairs loo.
No windows. In the dark.
They stand there just waiting to be taken out in the sunlight.
Occasional witness to visitors shitting and wiping their arses.

Alan comes walking though the beach café, coming up from the beach.

PATRICIA
Hell! Christ! Jesus! There's Alan. Bloody Hell!

MICHAEL
Alan? Who might he be that makes you swear so uncharacteristically?

PATRICIA
Hello you! What you doing here?

ALAN
Much the same as you I imagine.
Taking the sun?
Passing the time on a sunny Sunday afternoon?
And maybe even looking for you?
Where have you been the past three weeks and four days?

PATRICIA
Washing clothes, reading newspapers, worrying about my weight,
cutting my nails - the usual.

Michael, sensing tension, gets up to get coffee.

MICHAEL
OK then - I'll get us some coffee.

ALAN
Why thanks?

PATRICIA
Thank you Michael.
He takes his nearly cold. Three sugars.

Michael walks away among the tables and disappears into the coffee-house.

ALAN
Who's he and why didn't you introduce me?

PATRICIA
Didn't get a chance, did I?
You monopolised the time and the space with your anxieties.

ALAN
Why didn't you phone, write an email or indeed come and find me in person?
You have a bike. There is a tram. I have an address. What's his name?

PATRICIA

Michael.

ALAN

Who is he?

PATRICIA

Hey! You're sounding aggressive.

ALAN

I am jealous. Of course I'm jealous.
That you can be sitting in the sun on the beach
– on a relaxed Sunday afternoon – with your
shoes off - and not with me.
Me - who loves you,
Me - who swapped sex for love and got hit on
the head pretty hard.
And am moping about like a sick cow.

PATRICIA

Sick bull.

ALAN

Either. Whatever. What is gender at a time like
this?

PATRICIA

A great deal I'd say.

ALAN

Love - like sex - is at heart genderless.

PATRICIA

Tell me about it.

ALAN

You have sentenced me to misery of a
particular desperate kind.

PATRICIA

Alan – over-stretched dramatics.
We don't live in a heroic age - haven't you
noticed?

ALAN

No. I haven't noticed. My feelings are pretty
dramatic and probably heroic.
I have sorely missed you.

PATRICIA

Sorely? You have archaic words to run
alongside your archaic feelings.

ALAN

Jesus! What's archaic about my feelings for
you?

PATRICIA

You just want to fuck me.

ALAN

I surely do. I surely do.
I have the image of your delightful buttocks
constantly before my eyes
and the presence of your cunt in my world is
like the centre of the universe.

PATRICIA

Hey - it's only a piece of damp female anatomy
- no big deal.

ALAN

It's much bigger than a big deal to me.

PATRICIA

Ok. I admit your desire for my private parts
does turn me on.

ALAN

So can we fuck?

PATRICIA

Now? Here?

ALAN

If you want – let's walk into the dunes.

PATRICIA

We could do that – would that help? And for
how long?

ALAN

For as long as it takes.

PATRICIA

Then what?

ALAN

I want to live with you.

PATRICIA

In your dirty little apartment?

ALAN

If needs be.
But your clean little paradise of tourist posters
and holiday brochures would do as well.

PATRICIA

Alan, we have discussed this so often we are
wearing out the words for togetherness,
partnership, concubinage…

ALAN

I would never use that word.

PATRICIA

Isn't it interesting that we have never used
words like marriage and wedding?

ALAN

They would not be relevant would they?
They would hardly be relevant would they?
Would they?
Jesus - is that what you want – if it is - I readily
and madly agree.

PATRICIA

Ssshhhh - here comes Michael.

ALAN

Does he know I love you?

PATRICIA

God! Do we have to post up headlines?
Michael - this is Alan.
Alan - this is Michael.

MICHAEL

Alan - what is it that you readily and madly
agree to?

ALAN

Patricia has asked me to marry her.

MICHAEL

Really?

PATRICIA

No I have not.

MICHAEL

Is this a long time decision or a spur of the
moment thing?
Either way - I for one would object.

ALAN

What the fucking hell has it got to do with you?

MICHAEL
Well surprisingly enough - Patricia loves me.
She does not love you.
And marriage without love seems a paltry
business.

PATRICIA
Michael!?

MICHAEL
I am interested in Patricia's well-being.

PATRICIA
I did not know you could be so bourgeois.

MICHAEL
Neither did I - come to think of it.
A rival brings out the worst in me.

ALAN
A rival? You consider yourself a rival? A rival?
To me?

MICHAEL
I suppose I am now going to be dragged into
that role.

ALAN
OK. You over-weight supercilious freak – I
challenge you.

MICHAEL
Dear me. Traditional values. I suppose I have to
agree.

PATRICIA
Michael - he will hurt you.

ALAN
Patricia! That sounds like disloyalty.

PATRICIA
He is a swimming instructor.

MICHAEL
Is he really?

PATRICIA
Well - part-time swimming instructor.

MICHAEL
Well - maybe we could go and fight it out in the
water?

SECTION 23

BEACH FIGHT
DAY. EXTERIOR. SUNNY DAY. SUMMER.

Alan and Michael are fighting on the beach – just out of the tide-reach - scrabbling about, getting soaked with water and gritty with sand. They have gathered a small crowd – variously dressed in summer clothes, T-shirts, swimming costumes - who watch them dispassionately. Patricia is there, looking resigned and rather sad. A large burly man - Simon - in very skimpy yellow bathing trunks, addresses Patricia.

SIMON

What are they fighting about?

PATRICIA

A woman.

SIMON

Usual thing.

PATRICIA

Is it?

SIMON

Sex thing?

PATRICIA

Yes.

SIMON

Usual thing.

PATRICIA

Is it?

SIMON

How do you know it's a sex thing?
Looks to me like a possession thing.

PATRICIA

Really? That could be the same.
Possession of a woman?
Though it seems to me it's a sex thing.

SIMON

How do you know it's a sex thing?

PATRICIA

I am the woman.

SIMON

Really?
Good lord! They are fighting over you?

PATRICIA

Seems like it - and you needn't sound so surprised.

SIMON

Are you worth fighting over?

PATRICIA

You are not improving your concern. But it seems so.

SIMON

Yes, looking at you - I can see that.

PATRICIA

Thank you.

SIMON

Do you want me to join in?
You could be worth fighting for.

PATRICIA

No - two's enough. Three would be crowded.

SIMON
Which one do you favour?

PATRICIA
The fatter one.

SIMON
Really?
The least attractive.
And he's losing.

PATRICIA
Yes, seems so.

SIMON
It's strange isn't it? Men don't really
know how to fight anymore.
You don't often see men fighting over a
woman.
Least not like this.
Maybe they should do it more often.
Get some practice.
I would suggest your fatter one should
get in closer.
His body's soft and his arms are shorter.
He should try to smother his opponent
more.

PATRICIA
Perhaps you would like to tell him?

SIMON
He'll bruise, but maybe he can take the
punches.

PATRICIA
What punches?

I haven't seen a decent punch yet.
They are just scrabbling about.

SIMON
If you favour the fatter one - shouldn't
you intervene?
He's not doing so good.

PATRICIA
What use would I be?
Let them fight it out.
Let them get hurt. He's hurt me. They've
hurt me.

SIMON
Well there you go I suppose.
No wonder they are fighting - they
deserve it.
Let me buy you a brandy. Cheer you up.

SECTION 24

AFTER FIGHT CONVERSATION
Day. Exterior. Sunny Day. Summer.

Patricia and Alan and Michael with Simon in tow are back in the beach-café, drinking. Alan and Michael are gritty with sand, with torn jacket and trousers – both soaked through – both bruised – Alan with a developing black eye and a cut lip. Michael with blooded sand-scratches on his cheek and chin. They are the object of curiosity from the surrounding café drinkers.

PATRICIA
So?

ALAN
So what?

PATRICIA
Done your fighting?

ALAN
Yes.

PATRICIA
Settled everything?

ALAN
No! You bitch!

MICHAEL
Shut up. We've done that bit.

ALAN
You might have. I haven't.
I'm bleeding.

PATRICIA
It's superficial. Makes you look tough.

ALAN
What has been settled then?

MICHAEL
Very little.

ALAN
So we still have business to settle?

MICHAEL
Who would you say won?

ALAN
I did.

MICHAEL
Won the battle, but lost the war? She still loves me.

PATRICIA
Do I?
Fat, unfit and badly bruised?

MICHAEL
But not conquered.

ALAN
It was a foreseen thing.

MICHAEL
Was it? I wonder.

SIMON
I should leave this prick. He's washed up.

MICHAEL
Not really. I feel bruised but I confess I do feel invigorated

ALAN
Masochist.

MICHAEL
Yes, perhaps you're right.
You rarely - if ever - get a chance to fight like that.

SIMON
Like what? A fight between two scrapping women?

MICHAEL
I don't think we are asking for your opinion.

PATRICIA
(to Simon) I think you had better leave.

SIMON
You said you were pissed off with both of them.

ALAN
Really? Did you?

SIMON
That's what you said.

PATRICIA
I might have. See it from my point of view.

MICHAEL
Really?

PATRICIA
Wouldn't you be pissed off - in my shoes?
And fighting is not an overly bright way to solve the dilemma.

ALAN
I love you. And you don't love me.

MICHAEL
You love me and I don't love you.

SIMON
Triangle thing.

PATRICIA
Tedious really. Played out so very often - time and time and tedious time again.

MICHAEL
Though rarely nowadays physically.

PATRICIA
This time the three of us have made it look very simple.
Good Lord a classic triangle fight - out in the open.
On a beach.

SIMON
That fight didn't look very classic.

ALAN
Who is this guy?

PATRICIA
He bought me a coffee as a consolation prize.

ALAN
What ever happened I couldn't win.

MICHAEL
So he bought you a coffee?

PATRICIA
He offered me a brandy.
It's true I was shaking. Though I am all right now.

MICHAEL
Amazing! You jerk!

PATRICIA
Yes, it did cross my mind too that he wanted to take advantage of the situation.
After one brandy - another - and than a walk in the dunes.

ALAN
Bastard!

PATRICIA
Don't worry. Don't concern yourself. I just took a coffee instead.
I didn't want to complicate matters.

ALAN
Bastard!

SIMON
Hey mate! I am on your side.
At least you had a decent punch.
Didn't see you use it – but I could see it was there.

MICHAEL
Sycophant!

ALAN
Let's say it again - I think you had better be going.

SIMON
Why - you going to make me?
I am with the lady and you obviously are not.

MICHAEL
You are pushing your luck.

SIMON
The way I saw you fighting I don't think so.

PATRICIA
Let him stay.
His staying here sort of works. He can be a focus for your anger.
Because I don't want to be.
He can buy us all a brandy now we are safely out of the fighting zone.
You can stay if you buy us all a brandy.

ALAN
It could get expensive because we may need a second one, perhaps a third.

PATRICIA
Buy the bottle.

Simon leaves to buy brandy.

ALAN
Your jacket's ruined.

MICHAEL
So's your trousers.

PATRICIA
You drew quite a crowd.
All professional fight watchers, it seems.
They were full of advice.
Never before seen a fight in their lives.
Fights are getting rare.
There was a guy taking photographs.

ALAN
We should ask him for the photos – perhaps we could work out who won on points

MICHAEL
Still think it's unresolved eh?

PATRICIA
Does it need to be resolved?

MICHAEL
Perhaps.

PATRICIA
I tell you a way to resolve it.
You can both sleep with me and I can award
points on sexual satisfaction.

ALAN & MICHAEL TOGETHER
What!?

PATRICIA
I suppose when you think about it - it was
really all a sex thing.
Not really a love thing at all.

ALAN
Love is still lost on me.

PATRICIA
So let's resolve it on the sex thing.
I am after new experiences – here's one that is
unlikely to get repeated.
*(she points at the hotel behind them – about 400
metres away)*
It's an OK hotel. For a Dutch seaside.
Let's book a good room and resolve it.

MICHAEL
That's no resolve.

PATRICIA
Maybe we should ask our friend to come and
watch and award points.

ALAN
Then he can fuck you and we watch.
Consolation prize.

MICHAEL
Now you really are being crude.

PATRICIA
Nah! Couldn't imagine what he's got under
those Hawaiian briefs.

MICHAEL
Something very brief I imagine.

ALAN
Crude? Oh and what was your suggestion?

PATRICIA
Crude? I don't know - maybe - but you have to
agree I am the crux of all this.
I would quite like it resolved - than we can
come to a decision and move on.

ALAN
Move on - what do you mean "move on"?

PATRICIA
Well? The fighting apparently didn't prove
anything.
And I have to admit the sex with both of you
was good, even very good.
In different ways of course.

MICHAEL
(with sarcasm) "A white pencil laid over summer
plums"?

PATRICIA

(not letting him get away with his sarcasm) A chubby rabbit prick?

ALAN

(he snorts) Hey! We could compare notes – see which sloppy simile was most fitting.

PATRICIA

Maybe you could both learn something from one another?
I stayed here once with my dad – preacher's convention or something.
It's a fairly good hotel– as far as seaside holiday hotels go.
I remember there's a swimming pool in the basement – football teams sometimes stay here – there is a great communal shower bath.
Get showered. Clean up.
I'll book a room. A double-room. A treble-room in fact.

MICHAEL

No!

PATRICIA

No? Why not?
Go and wash the sand out of your ears.

ALAN

I love you.

PATRICIA

Come on!
Even if it was true I am afraid, you know Alan, that I don't love you.
Come on! We have been on and on and around and around this one for ages.

And I love this guy and he doesn't love me.
He is stupid enough to say he would be even prepared to live with me – but that's because who he is – he would do it for me and not for himself and I know it would be an utter disaster.
Unlike you or indeed like you - you would selfishly say "Live with me"
and you would hope for the best and it would not be the best.
If you love me, you wouldn't do it.
You only love you. And you especially love you loving.

MICHAEL

So what do we have left?

PATRICIA

Whatever else - I certainly love your pricks and what they can do for me. Do I settle for fucking with both of you forever?
Alternate Mondays? Only on your birthdays?
One in the morning and one in the afternoon.
Let's round things up and call it a day.
One last time.
Oh look - here's our benefactor.
(to Simon) You busy the next two hours?

SIMON

No.

PATRICIA

Come and be a referee.

SIMON

Of what?

PATRICIA

What shall we call it? A love match?

SIMON

What do I have to do?

PATRICIA

Don't look so alarmed. Watch us make love
and decide on a winner.

MICHAEL

Patricia - none of us is going to win.

PATRICIA

Look - we all entered this thing using sex to
find out about love.
You won. I lost
I won. You lost.
But no real wins. Were there any real losses?
Let's play the final round. Three in the ring.
And we have a referee.

SIMON

No.

PATRICIA

Why ever not?
You are a professional voyeur of other people's
miseries.
You watched these two slogging it out for love,
punching one another to pieces.
Come and watch other people's joys.

SIMON

Joys?
It's perverted.

PATRICIA

Oh dear. Are you one of those?
Come on. It's free. Most people would be
happy to come and watch.
No holds barred. Drink up and bring the bottle.

PART 8

SECTION 25

HOTEL SHOWER-ROOM
Day. Interior. Summer.

*Alan and Michael are in the hotel shower-bath on the
lower ground-floor, to wash off the grit and sand from
their fight on the beach. It is comparatively dark. There
is a rain-storm coming. Alan tries flicking the light
switch on and off – the light bulbs give off a low feeble
light. He gives up, carelessly starts to take off his damp,
sandy, torn suit of clothes.*

ALAN

What is this all about? She is a sensationalist.

MICHAEL

Is she?
She's just after experience - she's experience-
hungry.

*Now Michael switches the switch – same feeble light.
He gives up.*

ALAN

She was looking for love and I found it.

MICHAEL

Really?
With me she was looking for sex and found
love, she says.
But I think she's looking too hard.
You set her up, told her what to do, how to
behave, what to expect,
and found me to experiment with on the
rebound.
Sex and love.

When you really honestly think about it - what
is the difference?

ALAN

A great deal I'd say.

Alan carelessly takes off his shirt and socks

MICHAEL

It's evolutionary.

ALAN

Oh?

MICHAEL

It's a programming thing.

Michael carefully takes off his shirt and jeans.

ALAN

Oh?

MICHAEL

Darwin.
Evolutionary thing.
First and foremost, it's an animal thing -
practical and evolutionary.
Animals who bond are more likely to survive -
and not just survive for sex.
Bonded animals produce more successful
offspring. Hence - love.

ALAN

Not true - look at turtles.
They fuck in the sea – females leave their eggs
on a deserted beech at night.
Thousands and tens of thousands - millions
even - hatch out.
Successful offspring.

72

MICHAEL

And most of them get eaten.
Even before they reach the sea.
Less than five per cent survive to adulthood.
Bad parentage. No bonding.
Ends in wholesale slaughter.
Massive infanticide.
Not that bright – turtles.

ALAN

That's biological snobbism.
In their own way - in their own element -
turtles are very bright.
Animals don't have love. They just have sex -
which is apparently enough.

MICHAEL

As I said. And besides we are animals.

ALAN

With humans - is sex enough?

Alan and Michael both are naked. Michael turns on the taps and tests the temperature of the water, operating the shower-heads.

MICHAEL

We set this whole love thing up to excuse and
justify the appalling urgent push to procreate.
This creation thing is very very dangerous if
you want stability.
Massive over the top fucking produces
mayhem.
I saw it once at the zoo.

Michael, having found the correct water-temperature, turns to face Alan. Both men noticeably look at one another's bodies, and certainly at one another genitals.

MICHAEL

Six Mallard drakes – ingesting extra oestrogen
from gobbling white bread provided by ignorant
visitors, rape two mallard ducks with chicks, end
up pecking three chicks to death, and poking out
one duck's eye and drowning the other in their
manic eagerness to screw.
Ending up with four duck chick orphans with a
half blind surrogate mother.
I was distressed and appalled.
Disaster all round.
End of duck family life.
Repeat that universally - end of species.
For ducks - take the Siege of Orleans, the Sack
of Rome, March of the Red Army on Berlin.
Manic rape rape rape - leading to terminal
disaster.

They have soap and shampoo and start to wash and shower.

MICHAEL

One child in every ten is apparently conceived
outside monogamous partnerships.
Meaning one tenth of all mankind are bastards.

ALAN

In more ways than one. Which side are you
on?

MICHAEL

Our side. You because you love. Me because
I'm loved.
But no alarm is intended. It's arranged that
way. And it is necessary to keep a good stirred
up soup of genetic material.
But just to be on the same side, we invent a
thousand games and systems and agendas to

make fucking around less dangerous.
Love is just one of those things.

Alan grips his side in pain.

ALAN

Ouch!

Michael looks at Alan's body.

MICHAEL

You shave?

They both look down at Alan's shaven belly and genitals.

ALAN

I didn't before her.
I used to think it was a gay thing.
After her - I did. Her idea.
It turned her on. Now it turns me on.

Alan looks at Michael's shaven belly and genitals.

ALAN

As apparently you surely know.
So I suspect it turns you on.

MICHAEL

Yep! Her idea.
Though I can also see for her - your great
endowment is an advantage.

They both look at Alan's prick.

MICHAEL

Hereditary?

ALAN

Not that I remember - then again I never saw so
much of my father's prick – and never I think
with a hard on.

MICHAEL

So she's moulded us both at the core of
intimacy?

Alan looks miserable.

MICHAEL

Listen, Alan, there is no such thing as love.
There 's mutual attraction, there is mutual self
gratification.
Self defence, need for companionship, mutual
help society.
And Lust.
And if Lust succeeds then that breeds more
mutual dependency.
And a certain stimulus I certainly agree at the
sight of a big cock.
Like yours. Even for me.
You must have had fun over the years.

ALAN

If we could satisfactorily measure sexual fun, I
probably have had no more than you. Big cock
or not so big cock.

MICHAEL

And now you think love has hit the fan.

Alan looks downcast.

MICHAEL

If you can find someone who will fulfil your
sexual dreams with equal understanding - chew
your ear, bite your cock, lick your anus - and
won't back away, laugh or ridicule or expose
you to other's contempt then you are going to
survive better.

*The conversation is subtly shifting into a homoerotic
gear. Both realise it, but abstain from acknowledging it.*

MICHAEL
And the rest is programming.
And absolutely total and immense peer-group pressure.
The peer-group pressure is enormous.
We all conspire in it.
Love concepts were once upon a time anti-establishment – anti-your parents, anti-the church council, anti-sensible banking.

ALAN
Anti-sensible banking?

MICHAEL
Love is not a good financial investment.
Arranged marriages are a better bet for good finance.

ALAN
Rubbish! Love means commitment to the bitter end.

MICHAEL
Oh yeah?

ALAN
Couldn't be a better investment.

MICHAEL
Oh yeah?

There is a distant crash of thunder and then lightning lights up the dimly-lit shower-room.
After the lightning-flash it seems noticeably darker.

MICHAEL
Yesterday's anti-establishment behaviour become tomorrow's status quo.
He who is against the idea of loving is a total social outcast.

The invention of love has made the idea of love imperative.
If you don't love, or you are not loved, you are a social misfit, social pariah, outcast, a sad piece of social junk.
All our art, culture, science, politics, sociology, cinema, point to the love imperative.
TV's biggest obsession – you name it – sex and love.
Romeo and Juliet to Sex in the City – all exactly the same objective – the same rites of passage – the same as in "growing up in Samoa".

ALAN
Pardon me?

MICHAEL
Classic anthropology.
Sex ritualised and nothing special and stuffed into the sock called love.

Alan again winches at a muscle pain on his hip.

ALAN
Ouch!

Michael watches him with interest, looking at his bruised eye from the fight on the beech.

MICHAEL
Let's have a look at that eye.

He looks closely.

MICHAEL
This is going to be a big bruise tonight and you could have sand in it.

Michael rubs Alan's eyebrow. The first conscious physical touch.

ALAN

I'll live.
I wrenched my hip when I fell the second time.

MICHAEL

Let me massage it.

ALAN

You know how to do it?

MICHAEL

My father used to be a physiotherapist for
Ajax.

There is a flash of lightning and a thunder crash.
Michael massages Alan's hip.
Alan's prick begins to rise.

MICHAEL

I see you and your cock are getting prepared
for something?

ALAN

It's the hot water and the invigorating fight.

MICHAEL

Are you sure about that?

Michael too now has an erect penis. It is dark in the
shower-room with the rain-storm darkening the outside
world – though we can still see the expressions on the
men's faces and we can still see their bodies. The
lightning reflects on their wet bodies.

ALAN

Well - and what might your excuse be?

MICHAEL

(he laughs) The thunderstorm?

ALAN

(he smiles) I hated you and now I don't.

MICHAEL

So it could be perhaps a sign of release and
relief?
With Patricia finished?
Your love being a hopeless case?
Will you freak out if I hold your prick?

ALAN

Depends.

MICHAEL

On what?

ALAN

How you hold it?

Michael steps close to Alan and raises his hand to take
hold of his prick.
The phone on the wall in the shower-room rings. They
stare at the phone ringing.

MICHAEL

(he smiles) Saved by the bell?

ALAN

Decision deferred?

MICHAEL

We are called upon to perform.
You could take out your love for a final airing.

SECTION 26

HOTEL BEDROOM
DAY. INTERIOR WITH EXTERIOR VIEW. THUNDERSTORM. SUMMER.

Patricia and Alan and Michael experiment with love and sex in the second floor hotel bedroom over looking the dunes, the beach and the sea. The storm outside blows the curtains at the open window. The large double bed has side-tables with bedside lamps which are lit. Patricia is naked in the double-bed with the sheets covering her nakedness.

PATRICIA
What kept you?
I am insulted.

MICHAEL
We were still quarrelling over you.

PATRICIA
Oh!?

MICHAEL
About precedence.

ALAN
Where's the brandy-man?

PATRICIA
Absconded. Scared we had designs on him and his body.
(laughing) He left me a forwarding address.
In case we should need him another time.
Said he should be better prepared.
I wonder how?
I think he just could not believe we were serious.

ALAN
Me too.
I just don't believe this is going to happen.

PATRICIA
Why not?

ALAN
It's a literary device engineered for a film.

PATRICIA
The hotel is taking care of your clothes.
Repaired and laundered and dry-cleaned in three hours.
So we have three hours - minimum.

MICHAEL
Will that be time enough?

PATRICIA
It's my party. I decide the agenda.
And I'll cry if I want to.
Two against one and if it gets nasty I will certainly lose.

MICHAEL
So you think of it as a contest?

ALAN
How about a contest between him and me, and not us against you?
Points and a knock-out blow. Extra points for elegance.

Thunder and lightning at the window.

MICHAEL
And of course everything below the belt.
And clinches to be encouraged and made desirable.
Handicaps to be considered

ALAN
I have no handicap except love.

MICHAEL
Surely that's an advantage?

ALAN
Under these conditions I think not.

PATRICIA
However, it goes I am trusting you are civilised
human beings and won't get nasty. Or vulgar.
Or at least not excessively vulgar.
A little vulgarity can be fun.
And I will have no regret for the missing
referee.
And I am - as you can see - a consenting female
over 18.
In fact, over 33 - age of Christ and Alexander at
death.
And more than eager to leave that age behind if
only to banish those two ever omnipresent
ghosts hovering over my head.
First I need a presentation.
Let's see you present your weapons.
I enjoyed seeing them apart.
Let me see if I enjoy seeing them together.

*Alan and Michael look at one another and then open
their towelling dressing-gowns to show Patricia their
pricks. Patricia throws off the bed sheet to reveal her
nakedness. She grabs their pricks and pulls them
towards the bed.*
*They make love in a thunderstorm. They both kiss and
caress her body, Alan at her head and shoulders and
breasts, Michael at her waist, hips and thighs.*
*But it is Alan who copulates with her first. Their
copulation is quick and energetic. Michael does not
watch but buries his face in Patricia's neck and hair,
and he holds her breasts.*

*They reach orgasm together. Then it is Michael's turn.
Michael and Patricia together make love more slowly.
Alan holds Patricia's shoulders and watches. Michael
and Patricia arrive at orgasm at different times,
Patricia first, then Michael.*

*Having finished, they sit and lie naked in the sheets.
Then with the thunder crashing, they stand and move to
the verandah over looking the sea in the thunderstorm.
Everybody has left the beach. They watch the storm. As
do we. Patricia stares at the rain and accurately
describes it.*

PATRICIA
Steel pins and silver rings.

SECTION 27

AFTERMATH IN THE HOTEL SHOWER
DAY. INTERIOR. SUMMER

Patricia and Alan and Michael take a combined shower. Michael soaps Patricia's back.
Alan washes his own hair, then soaps Michael's hair.
Patricia takes the shampoo and washes her own hair.
Both men rinse one another's hair. Patricia notes the gathering interest between the two men.

PATRICIA
I'm finished. I am going to leave.

MICHAEL
Why don't we catch up in the restaurant?

ALAN
Let's have dinner.

PATRICIA
We could indeed.

MICHAEL
See you there in half an hour.

Patricia leaves, wrapped in a towel.
When she has gone, the men wait a few minutes watching one another and then embrace, arms around one another's shoulders.

SECTION 28

HOTEL BEDROOM
DAY. INTERIOR WITH EXTERIOR VIEW. AFTERNOON-EVENING. SUMMER.

Patricia in the large hotel room the three shared, sits on the bed of crumpled sheets and stares at the rain still falling outside on the sea. Naked, she combs out her hair. The rain is ceasing. Large rain-drops gather on the verandah roof and then fall to the wooden verandah floor. She holds out her hand to catch them. She is weeping. She mingles the rain-drops with her tears.

SECTION 29

MALES MAKE LOVE IN THE SHOWER
Day. Interior. August.

The men are embracing in the shower. They part and stare at one another.

MICHAEL

And?

ALAN

And?

MICHAEL

Not so much was at stake for me as it was for you.

ALAN

She came slowly for you.

MICHAEL

Love – she says.

ALAN

Yeah?

MICHAEL

Don't look so glum.

ALAN

Maybe you've got it wrong and I am not looking glum.
But perplexed.

Both men are aroused.

MICHAEL

How's that? Don't answer. I am seeing the answer.
Delayed excitement?

ALAN

No.

MICHAEL

Renewed excitement?

ALAN

You were impressive.
Easily impressive.
No wonder she loved you.

MICHAEL

Me?
You were impressive too.
We both were impressive.

ALAN

Showing off to one another?

MICHAEL

Stimulated by one another?

ALAN

Well – Hell, what have we got to prove?

MICHAEL

Come here. Let's find out.

ALAN

You're fat.
I like the fact that you're fat.

MICHAEL

I'm plump. 93 kilos.

ALAN

And the rest. 98.
Let's knock it down to 90 for a start.

We don't want you dying on us.
(he touches Michael's body)
You could lose it here and here. But no more.

He holds Michael's prick

ALAN
It's bigger than it was in there.

MICHAEL
Do I remind you of her?

ALAN
No. Yes. In a way. No.

MICHAEL
You love her, loved her, loved her body - you
said.

ALAN
Wasn't that what was all the fight was about?

MICHAEL
It was.

ALAN
Could it then be some sort of transference?

MICHAEL
You going to fight me again over transference?

ALAN
If it helps. No I am not.

MICHAEL
Because you might be fighting her?

ALAN
No. Yes. No.

MICHAEL
Fighting might help?

ALAN
It might

MICHAEL
Bastard!

ALAN
Really?

They fight clumsily on the tiled shower-bath floor – a
scrambling fight that moves to love-making.

SECTION 30

HOTEL RESTURANT
DAY. INTERIOR WITH EXTERIOR VIEW. AFTERNOON-EVENING. AUGUST.

*Alan and Michael, dressed after the shower, with still wet
hair, enter the empty restaurant –the storm has abated –
distant rumbling – clear evening red skies over the
Western seas.*
*Alan picks up a note left on a table, from Patricia. He
reads it and passes it to Michael.*
*Michael reads the letter out aloud. We see the note and
recognise the handwriting.*

You see - my experiment worked.
I was absolutely right.
We found a way out.

All three of us.

                       ALAN
It's her handwriting alright. Which fills me
with nostalgia.
Look at that beautifully squashed letter b.
She's left.

                   MICHAEL
I don't think we can be surprised.

*They look around at the rather forlorn empty
restaurant.*

PART 9

SECTION 31

ALAN'S APARTMENT
NIGHT. INTERIOR. SUMMER.

Michael and Alan are sitting on a settee in Alan's untidy apartment, drinking beer from the bottle. Both wear T-shirts covered in handwritten calligraphy-graffiti - but are otherwise naked. They have just been making love. They are illuminated by the light of a flickering muted TV.

MICHAEL
How did you meet her?

ALAN
Is this going to be a post mortem?
I thought we had made a new beginning?

MICHAEL
So how did you meet Patricia?
We might truly need to lay the ghost.

ALAN
We met in a supermarket.

MICHAEL
Supermarket?
Once upon a time most people met one another on a dance floor.
Now they meet in supermarkets.

ALAN
She gave me her handwriting. A grocery list.
Her Bs were squashed.

He gets up, naked from the waist down - and walks away out of the TV light into the darkness of the room. He returns with Patricia's supermarket grocery list framed.

ALAN
Graphology.
I dropped out of art school.
Only thing I really liked and enjoyed there was calligraphy.
Handwriting as an art form.
Too grand to call it calligraphy.
Just the mark of text on paper.
Handwritten text.

They lie on the bed and look at Patricia's handwriting.

ALAN
It was far too little to be allowed to remain in art school for.
I left. I was a graffiti-artist on and off for three years. Got scars to prove it.
I just like to see texts on buildings.
Text on architecture.

We see a montage of Alan's faded graffiti-tags on the Amsterdam buildings he lists.

ALAN
My tag is still on the Heineken Building in Ferdinand Bolstraat,
On the Old Post Office Stedelijk, in the Van Gogh Museum basement, at the back of the Concertgebouw, near the artist's entrance …

Alan become excited at his list of achievements. He lies on the bed on his back, showing his naked body to his lover.

..... on the walls of the Schouwburg, on Platform Six of Amsterdam Central Station, on the Westerkerk where Rembrandt was buried, the old Hell's Angels Club near the prison, the Oude Kerk in the red light district, the Amstel Hotel under the water-line with water-proof paint, the Olympic stadium, the Anne Frank House - she tagged inside it afterall in 1945, and I tagged me outside in 2011 .... and the Amsterdam Hilton where John and Yoko fucked and Herman Brood threw himself out of a window.
After seven years, Amsterdam is still full of my texts. My favourite is under the drawbridge near the Hermitage.
Not at all easy to do from a moving barge.

He holds up the framed Patricia grocery list.

ALAN
I liked her squashed Bs.
All my Bs in those days were squashed too.
When I lay on top of her, all her Bs were squashed as well.
Breasts, belly, buttocks.
I liked that.
(he sighs)
So that's me. How about you?

MICHAEL
Cinema. I met Patricia in the Tuschinski Cinema

ALAN
I never took Patricia to a cinema.
She is afraid of the dark.

MICHAEL
Was she?
She loves the cinema.

ALAN
Never said.

MICHAEL
I met her crying in the dark.
On her own.

ALAN
Crying in the dark?
Well - she was not crying over me.

MICHAEL
I am sure - now I think of it - she certainly was.
Though I didn't know it at the time.

ALAN
She was clever. I never knew you existed.

MICHAEL
I knew you did.

ALAN
Fucking Hell, you did!?
That makes it worse.

MICHAEL
How's that?

ALAN
If you knew I was around – you should have backed off!

MICHAEL
How long did you know her?

ALAN

Five months.
Twenty weeks.
Six fucks a week. One hundred and twenty fucks.

MICHAEL

More than enough to make a baby.
They say - averaging out – it takes fifty fucks to make a baby.
One baby for every fifty copulations. Not so many.

ALAN

You?

MICHAEL

Since maybe May.

ALAN

Fucks?

MICHAEL

Didn't count.
Certainly a lower average than you.

ALAN

So how come you were on your own in the cinema?

MICHAEL

I like the dark.

ALAN

You were being predatory?

MICHAEL

No.
They say you are permitted to fall in love two and a half times.

Half a love is permitted - though the statistics are arrived at by averaging.
The first time was all calf love and experimental.
Aided by youth and drinking and various species of contempt for political opinions. And there was a mother-in-law in there somewhere.
Didn't help that I fucked the mother-in-law at a church christening.
Or rather she fucked me.
The second engagement was destroyed by a car crash.
Couldn't come to terms with the pathologically wounded.
She was taken off my hands very quickly by a hospital car park attendant which lead to her engagement to a radiologist.
But that is sometime long ago now.
If pushed and I was feeling confessional I would say experience has persuaded me that continued success in love won't happen.
Or will happen only long enough to conceive, sire and set a child going.
The seven-year itch is about right.
It's Darwinian - about the right time for the biological cycle to make and bring up a walking talking child and set it free.

ALAN

Seven is a bit young to launch a child into the world.

MICHAEL

The seven years would have been good enough in man's evolutionary beginnings.
Apes are more than grown up and independent by age seven.

Hence the seven-year itch.
We were related-apes for a very long time –
hence the deep impression the seven years
made – we still have the itch – built in.
Neolithic man was fertile at seven? Can that be
true?
Dead by 14.

ALAN
You don't believe in everlasting love?

MICHAEL
The very closest I got to the love-trap was
sprung open by that car crash.
(Michael looks melancholic. He lowers his voice.)
Delayed shock, they said.
Everyone said it was my fault.
It was not - but I let everyone believe it.
I moped about but nobody dies of a broken heart.
Does anyone die of a broken heart?

ALAN
Only on stage or in a movie.

MICHAEL
What do you miss most?

ALAN
Entry into a female body.
My prick being gripped by a moist warm cunt.
I thought this - us - you and I - was only a sex
thing - mutual orgasm anytime you want – no
holds barred - and I would soon go back to
women.

MICHAEL
Why not see this out?

To make sure you have got over Patricia and
then …

ALAN
… and then?

MICHAEL
We'll see if the sex thing burns itself out.
…. and then we'll see.

ALAN
You'll see?
I do not think I want to be in a hurry.

MICHAEL
We could try it for seven years.

ALAN
And then let the itch decide?

They embrace.

PART 10

DOCTOR'S SURGERY
Day. Interior. Morning. Autumn.

*Patricia, wearing a white T-shirt pulled down to cover
her thighs …and a white bra - is lying naked from rib-
cage down to her toes (head right of frame) horizontal to
the frame in a warm orange-lit surgery on a white
sheeted pallet in front of her friend and doctor, Diana,
(wearing an opened white house-coat) who is seated
behind her – both are drinking coffee in large white cups
with saucers. Behind Diana is a large mirror that reflects
Diana's back and only the naked part of the body of
Patricia, who is sometimes balancing her coffee cup on
her belly where there is no evidence of pregnancy.*

DIANA
You are pregnant.

PATRICIA
That much could be obvious.
Three months, no periods. Much vomiting.

DIANA
Pregnant intentionally?

PATRICIA
Yes, and no. No and yes.
I was experimenting.
No deliberate protection and curious to feel
free of it.
It was indeed - as I sort of half expected -
liberating.
Sexual unprotection as a sort of lottery.
Letting my system make the decisions.

DIANA
And your body take huge risks.

PATRICIA
Are they so huge?
My body is designed to make babies – all of it -
cunt, tits, hips, sexy legs, mouth, sexy buttocks,
sweet soprano voice, long silky dyed blond
hair, glitzy eyes …

DIANA
Who are you describing?

PATRICIA
Me … and, come to think of it - without the
dyed blonde hair - you.
Go with the flow, no denial, open out, let the
juices flow, do what my body is designed and
supposed to do.

DIANA
You should think with your head and not with
your cunt.

PATRICIA
I wasn't aware that a cunt could think.

DIANA
More's the pity.

PATRICIA
I have to admit my cunt felt things very well
indeed even if it did not think them.
The cunt experience and the to-be results
certainly match.
Success both times - nine months apart? A
good fuck and a good baby.

DIANA
Should we not wait and see?

PATRICIA
Good Lord. You actually sound a little jealous?
Are you a little jealous?

DIANA
I thought you wanted to see the world, climb
Mount Everest, learn Mandarin, visit the China
Deep with George Clooney in a bathysphere.

PATRICIA
I do and I still will.

DIANA
Oh!? Should we not wait and see?

PATRICIA
This was no a dribbling experience, Diana,
enacted in a dark corner with hesitation and guilt.
It was a Niagara experience boldly undertaken.
In a storm.

DIANA
A storm?

PATRICIA
Lashings of water – "silver daggers and
splashing rings".
Noise to smash your ear-drums - and flashes of
bright white light.

DIANA
My my!

PATRICIA
Good eh?

What shall I eventually tell the little blighter?
"You were conceived in a fury of "sturm und
drang".
"You were conceived in a melodrama".

DIANA
He will be impressed.
Father?

PATRICIA
You do not need to know.

DIANA
Does he, the father, need to know??

PATRICIA
Oh yes they do.

DIANA
They?

PATRICIA
Sexual un-protection as a sort of lottery.
Lottery with my body - giving my body the
right to choose.
I gave it choices. This one? That one?

DIANA
More then than one?

PATRICIA
Absolutely!

DIANA
Patricia!

PATRICIA
Am I in danger?

DIANA
Not obviously. Maybe we should make tests?

Patricia laughs.

PATRICIA
Because there was more than one, we should automatically make tests?

DIANA
More than one suggests some irresponsibility.

PATRICIA
Does it?
Surely not on their part?

DIANA
And therefore perhaps carelessness on yours?

PATRICIA
Does it?
Diana - what prejudices!

DIANA
Do they both? … is it only "both", isn't it - or were there more …?

PATRICIA
Both will do. Two was enough.

DIANA
Do they both know there is another?

PATRICIA
Certainly they do

DIANA
How's that?

PATRICIA
Because they were both there at the same time.

DIANA
What?!

PATRICIA
And they both got so excited, they are now lovers.

DIANA
What!?

PATRICIA
(mocking) I have been cast aside. Abandoned. Repudiated.
I sought love with both of them and they found it with one another.

DIANA
God!

PATRICIA
A modern story, I think.

DIANA
So modern - it goes further.

PATRICIA
Oh!?

DIANA
You are expecting twins.

PATRICIA
What!?

DIANA
Your turn to say "What!?"
I am so glad I can still shock and surprise you.

PATRICIA

Jesus! Twins? That was unexpected –
Though come to think of it - why not?
It has a nice sort of symmetry.
Two for two.

DIANA

You want to know the sex?

PATRICIA

Go on. Tell me.

DIANA

Male.

PATRICIA

Yep! It figures - two more little pricks in the
world.

PART 11

SECTION 33

CAFÉ TERRACE - ANNOUCEMENT OF BIRTH
Day. Exterior. Afternoon. Spring.

A very pregnant Patricia is sitting in the Spring sunshine on a café terrace accompanied by two suitcases – her feet up on a chair – newspaper on her lap. Alan and Michael arrive, walking down the street backlit by an early Spring sun.

ALAN

Jesus!

MICHAEL

Patricia!

PATRICIA

Good morning gentlemen. Glad you could come.

MICHAEL

You are looking very healthy.

ALAN

And very pregnant.

PATRICIA

Well – your surprise and your eyes are worth watching.
They say health and pregnancy go together.
And you - are you both still together?

MICHAEL

Yes.

ALAN

Thanks of course to you.

MICHAEL
(pointing to the pregnant belly)
You are still experimenting I see?

PATRICIA
(with mocking self-irony)
Yes. Never an idle moment.
Curious how it all works.
Eager for experience.
A first time for everything.

Alan and Michael sit down at Patricia's table.

ALAN

And who – may we ask - is the father?

PATRICIA

You may certainly ask because you both are.

MICHAEL

Pardon?

ALAN

What?

PATRICIA

Well one of you is.
Unless fertilisation is uniquely different in your case.
And in this human supermarket (patting her belly) there is one for both of you.

ALAN

Pardon?

PATRICIA

Which is for who - will have to be up to you.

I suggest joint responsibility.
In later life I am certain that is what they will want.
Do you ever separate twins? I doubt it. You certainly try not to.
And you have to be there at the birth – witnessing that particular act finishes what you have begun.
You dipped your pricks in the holy receptacle.
Now you hold out your hands to receive what comes out.
Complete life cycle. It will bond you to your sons.

MICHAEL

Sons?

PATRICIA

Two of them for two of you.

MICHAEL

How do you know?

ALAN

And how do you know that we are responsible?

PATRICIA

Come on! Don't insult me! What do you think I am?
World's worst innocent or world's worst whore?
You always were, at heart, a little shit, Alan.

MICHAEL

Well Patricia – in self-protection - tutored by you – the title "self-advertising experimenter" was always on the propaganda table.

PATRICIA

This (patting her belly) does not strike me as merely propaganda.
This is the real thing. No virtual baby this. (she corrects herself) These.
And they have certainly been on the move for four weeks.
So they are certainly alive and kicking.
I have my bags packed and the hospital is down the road.
I am overdue and I am going to be induced.
I want you to be there.
Coming? (She begins to gather her possessions to go)

ALAN

No!

MICHAEL

Patricia?

PATRICIA

Come on. You can carry my suitcases. One each.
How could you ever possibly be doing something more important that witnessing the birth of your sons?

SECTION 34

BIRTH OF TWINS
Night. Interior. Sprring.

*Patricia is laid up in a birthing bed in a private ward –
with intravenous drips, and various medical aids,
having received the necessary treatments to induce the
baby, she is now Mother Earth, ready to give birth.*

PATRICIA
Something old, something new?
The something old would be this – my body.
Both of you in your former love life would be
familiar with my private parts.
The something new we will have to wait for.
Make yourselves comfortable. The wait could
be several hours.
Babies prefer to come at night. When it's dark
and cosy.
Get scrubbed and wear plastic hats and don't
touch anything you shouldn't.
Whilst the needles and pins and sticking plaster
do their work - you can regale me with stories
of your mutual love.

MICHAEL
Stop mocking.

PATRICIA
You must find it really ironic - both of you - to
have found between the two of you - what I
was so desperately looking for.

SECTION 35

HOSPITAL WARD PREPARATIONS ROOM
Night. Interior. Spring.

*Alan and Michael, wearing gowns and plastic hats and
plastic-covered shoes, are making love in a sideroom of
the hospital. The room is stored with hospital
apparatus, oxygen cylinders, etc. Alan, his buttocks
very visible, is taking Michael from the rear. They
collapse on the bed. They lie side by side.*

MICHAEL
We have a large enough apartment for a family.
Two spare rooms. Though the motorbike will
have to go.
And we'll have to set traps for the mice.
Can't lay poison down with children around.

ALAN
We have a cleaning lady.

MICHAEL
She hates babies.
We earn enough - well I do - you layabout.
But given the simplest push – with your
qualifications - you could earn twice as much
as me.

ALAN
We can set up the company properly.

*Michael gets up and goes to the window and looks out
at the dark hospital gardens and the lights of the city
beyond. He wears an open shirt, with his plastic hat
and gown on, but is naked from the navel down. They
are on the sixth floor.*

MICHAEL

I was born in this hospital.
And this is the hospital where they brought the mangled body of Margaret back after the crash.

Alan joins Michael at the window – like Michael he also exposes his belly and genitals to the world but wears his plastic hospital hat and gown.
A shot from outside – two semi-naked men looking out into the darkness. Alan has a red prick, red from its recent activity.

MICHAEL

Now it all depends on what happens next.

ALAN

A modern hospital. A healthy mother.
What could go wrong?

HOSPITAL LOUDSPEAKER FEMALE VOICE

Attention please: Will Michael and Alan please go to Birthroom 26 where their wife has gone into labour.

ALAN

That's going to start a riot.

MICHAEL

Did you hear them giggling?

They start to put on their underwear and trousers and make themselves presentable.

ALAN

Birthroom 26? – how many babies born tonight?

MICHAEL

Don't you think it's curious to hear both our names shouted out together in public?

SECTION 36

HOSPITAL WARD
Night. Interior. Spring.

Alan and Michael witness the birth of Patricia's twins. They become emotionally involved and excited.

SECTION 37

HOSPITAL WARD
DAY. INTERIOR. SPRING.

Assisted by nurses, Patricia breast-feeds, one child to each breast.
All three talk.

ALAN

So what now?

MICHAEL

Well - the obvious question we have all been waiting to ask needs answering.

PATRICIA

Oh what could that be I wonder?

MICHAEL

Who is responsible - who exactly is the father?

PATRICIA

Oh that. Does it matter?

MICHAEL

It could do - out there in the world.

ALAN

Do you know?

PATRICIA

Do I want to know?

ALAN

What sort of an answer is that?

MICHAEL

You knew they would be twins?

PATRICIA

Yes, I did

MICHAEL

One each?

ALAN

What does that mean?

PATRICIA

One for each of you.

ALAN

It doesn't work like that.

PATRICIA

It might have done in the old days.

ALAN

In the old days one of us would be dead.

MICHAEL

Slaughtered as a point of honour.

PATRICIA

Not necessarily.
Depends where you lived.

ALAN

I bet you one of us would be dead.

MICHAEL

We are getting away from the point.
Who is the father?

PATRICIA

I don't know.

95

ALAN
Come on - every woman knows.

PATRICIA
Does she?

ALAN
We could very easily find out.

PATRICIA
We could. Go on - make the test.

MICHAEL
Do we want to?

ALAN
Do you want to?

PATRICIA
What a strange idea.

MICHAEL
It will break the tradition of one hundred thousand years.

ALAN
Everyone wants to know who the father is.

PATRICIA
Do we?

ALAN
Human nature.

PATRICIA
You mean like "common sense" which is neither common nor sense.
Human nature is often not human and often not natural.

ALAN
What the Hell is it then?

PATRICIA
It's tradition, it's easy, it's protocol, it's received wisdom.
It's inbuilt machismo, it's guilt, it's mother-in-law stuff.

MICHAEL
If we are both the fathers – you have got two mothers-in-law.

PATRICIA
And I don't want to know either of them.

ALAN
We could find out and force the truth on you.

PATRICIA
Go on then. I'll be gone by then.

MICHAEL
And once the genie's out of the bottle you can't put it back.
And you'd know forever.

PATRICIA
That's true.
So that's what you are going to do?

MICHAEL
Not necessarily. What do you mean "you'll be gone by then?"

ALAN
I bet you'll find out eventually.

PATRICIA
Why should I?
Who's going to tell me?

ALAN
(indicating the babies) They will want to know.

PATRICIA
Will they?

MICHAEL
Not necessarily. What do you mean "you'll be gone by then?"

ALAN
There might be a medical emergency where it is important – imperative – life-saving - to know.

MICHAEL
And they'll suggest we should know because it'll save lives.

ALAN
Hereditary diseases.

PATRICIA
Have you got any?

ALAN
Not that I know of.

PATRICIA
Hartsfield's syndrome?

ALAN
What's that?

MICHAEL
Huntingdon's Chorea.

ALAN
You have to be super-brainy to get that.

PATRICIA
That's ruled you out then.

MICHAEL
Porphyria?

PATRICIA
George III.

ALAN
Asthma?

PATRICIA
Eczema?

MICHAEL
Big feet?

PATRICIA
Hardly life-threatening.

ALAN
Longevity?

PATRICIA
Desirable characteristic.

ALAN
Rhesus negative?

PATRICIA
Oh yeah? That one is up to me.

HIV? If either of you are HIV I am getting a
pistol to shoot you both dead.

ALAN

Not a problem.

PATRICIA

How do you know?
You both sleep around a lot.

MICHAEL

Patricia, that is what we both don't do.

PATRICIA *(to Alan)*

You've certainly had a past life of sleeping
around.
With a prick like yours it would have been
criminal not to.

ALAN

We would use condoms.

PATRICIA

With these two *(indicating babies)* you didn't.

ALAN

That's different?

PATRICIA

I see.
So I am a lady of easy virtue?
And you duped me? Come on.
I remember that fuck like it was yesterday.
There was thunder.

MICHAEL

There has always been thunder.

Patricia – you deliberately haven't answered me.
What do you mean "you'll be gone by then?"

PATRICIA

I have plans.

MICHAEL

What plans?

PATRICIA

Wait and see.

SECTION 38

PUBLIC HOSPITAL WARD
DAY. INTERIOR. SPRING.

*The men have brought flowers, drink, fruit, newspapers,
chocolates.
They each hold a swaddled baby – both babies are fast
asleep.*

MICHAEL

Well - say we agree not to know who the father
is?

ALAN

What then?

PATRICIA

Well what then then?
You are obviously capable of being good
fathers.
In my pains and travails last night I watched
you both – you were both bowled over with
what you had accomplished.
As fathers.
You could manage.

MICHAEL

We all could manage together.

PATRICIA

What - in some sort of ménage a trois?
No!

ALAN

How then?

PATRICIA

Wouldn't work.

MICHAEL

Would look very funny in the world.
Bad for the child – *(correcting himself)* -
children.

PATRICIA

You see - you are looking after their care and
mental health already - first base – probably the
most important really - wouldn't take you much
to learn the rest.
Are you going to volunteer to look after them?

MICHAEL

And you?

PATRICIA

Well I've done the love bit - didn't work – did it?
And the sex bit - again – well of course it did
work – didn't it?
Then there was the pregnancy bit - that was
lonely.

MICHAEL

You should have …

PATRICIA

I should have what?
Paid for an abortion? Screamed and shouted?
Moped? Threatened? Become melancholy?
Suffered depression? Committed suicide?
And now there's this baby bit.
And there's the milk-feeding bit – you
remember these tits don't you.
Now I am feeling they are de-sexualised.
Become merely functional – do they still
interest you?
In your newly earned sexual freedoms - breasts
don't figure, do they?

So I have done all those bits.
Now how about you doing a bit?
Well – it was all good experience - and now I'll move on.

MICHAEL
Figuratively speaking?

PATRICIA
Pardon me?
I am thinking "realistically speaking".
You both know - I've always wanted to be a professional human being and there's still a great deal to try out.

ALAN
My God!

PATRICIA
No.
We've been through that one so many times already - remember my father is a priest.
I am now 33 plus one.
Age of Christ and Alexander at death. Plus one.
Maybe having babies in a way is like having a death in the family.
It's a big marker in the life stakes.
I've done my bit on earth - passed on the genes.
All that what necessary.
You've said the only thing we've here for is to make babies - I've done it.
Made successful babies – two of them - over-succeeded in fact my 1.2 allowance.
They are successful - one's got a cold at the moment but otherwise they are successful.
All the right bits in all the right places.
Only thing we don't know yet is if they are fertile.
Babies are only really successful if they can make babies.

Continuity.
Otherwise dead end.
We've done our bit.
We are among the only fifty percent of the human race who reproduce themselves.

MICHAEL
Suppose then that they fail.

PATRICIA
Suppose.
They're very lucky - they have two daddies to look after them.
They are half again as lucky as most.

ALAN
Bottle-fed?

PATRICIA
Come on.

MICHAEL
After being breast-fed?

PATRICIA
I bet both of you were bottle-fed.

MICHAEL
Does it show?

ALAN
I bet we weren't.

MICHAEL
I was.

PATRICIA
You see.

ALAN
Come to think of it I was too.

PATRICIA
Case proven.
You don't need these *(breasts)* anymore.
They don't need these any more.
I'll pack them away, put them in storage and
then bring them out again the next time I want
to fall in love or want sex,
and then I can re-sexualise them again.

ALAN
They'll need you.

PATRICIA
Will they?
How do you know that – because you are going
to tell them?

MICHAEL
They'll need someone.

PATRICIA
That may be true.

ALAN
Come on it's fucking true.

PATRICIA
Well you'll do.

ALAN
Are you being very heartless?

PATRICIA
Well maybe in the state of things, in the way of
the world, conventionally it could be the usual
accusation.

ALAN
Don't you love them?

PATRICIA
Sure.

MICHAEL
Sure?

PATRICIA
Sure.
I must go for a pee before I go.

*She takes off the bed-clothes and she is dressed under
the sheets.*

ALAN
God!

PATRICIA
Well - in the circumstances I got dressed.
I thought it would be sensible.
No hanging around   with you two watching
me put my knickers on etc.
Keep watching them – it'll be practise - you'll
be safe here.
I'll only be a minute.
Pull the bell if you need a nurse to hold your
hand.
I am going for a pee and to put my face on.
You could ring for some tea. That would be a
nice idea.

Patricia leaves the ward.

SECTION 39

THE FATHERS TALK
Day. Interior. Approaching Thunderstorm. Spring.

> ALAN
> She can't be serious. It's a ruse.

> MICHAEL
> Why should it be a ruse?

> ALAN
> Is it legal? Can she be arrested?

> MICHAEL
> Can we be arrested?

> ALAN
> We know nothing about all this.

> MICHAEL
> All parents are amateurs.
> What is a professional parent?

> ALAN
> A mother who's had ten children?

> MICHAEL
> Not necessarily.

> ALAN
> She's brave and bold now - but she'll be back

> MICHAEL
> Why should she be back?

> ALAN
> Come on - mother love after nine months in the
> womb - inseparable bond.

> MICHAEL
> You've been seeing too many movies.

> ALAN
> You know I hate the cinema.

> MICHAEL
> Then too much Californian TV.

> ALAN
> They'll be paperwork. "Are you the father sir?"

> MICHAEL
> Could be.

> ALAN
> "What does that mean sir?"

> MICHAEL
> You needn't worry about those sorts of things
> these days.
> No stigma.

> ALAN
> And then they would make tests and we would
> know.

> MICHAEL
> Not if we made a fuss.

> ALAN
> Are we going to make a fuss?

*Patricia returns, hair brushed, face on, looking sexy
and desirable.*

> ALAN
> We've been talking.

PATRICIA

Sounds good.

I've been peeing.

Thank God I don't have to worry about my pee anymore.

What have you been talking about?

MICHAEL

Parenthood.

PATRICIA

Very good. You will be very good I am sure.

ALAN

Only we think it's all a joke

PATRICIA

Am I laughing?

ALAN

Yes, I think you are?

PATRICIA

Well inside I might be I suppose, to tell you the truth.

ALAN

So aren't you going to stay with them through thick and thin?

PATRICIA

I can send you postcards and they'll be reading them by the time they are seven.

ALAN

There's that seven thing again. Everything happens at seven apparently.

PATRICIA

Well better then than at 33.

And up till then, you can read them the postcards.

ALAN

Come on.

PATRICIA

No. I don't think, Alan, there is any "come on", in this case, at this time.

If there are papers to fill out I'll do the necessary, but by this time next week I want at the very least to be in Bogotá.

MICHAEL

Bogotá!?

ALAN

Why there for Christ's sake?

PATRICIA

It's a start. I have always been curious.

ALAN

So you'll take a break?

PATRICIA

Don't you think I need a break? Child-bearing is no holiday.

MICHAEL

And then you'll be back? And you expect us to hold the fort?

PATRICIA

Michael, with children, you are going to have to hold the fort forever.

And there are two of you.

Good jobs.

Well – in your cases I suppose they could be good jobs.
Save yours *(to Michael)* is boring – and yours *(to Alan)* – well, I don't know.
What are you doing now Alan? Washing-up in a Chinese restaurant?
Paper-boy to a bankrupt newspaper mogul?
Tram-driver?
Still picking up pocket-money from non-swimmers?
OK please don't tell me. I confess that I am not very interested – you know that.
But think of it, you could have a decent double income.
Pay for a nanny.
They start going to school in four years' time, you know.
Put their names down as soon as you can. It's a crowded world.
Get married.
One of you could get married.
Both of you could get married.
You've both had experience with women.
You know how it works.
Pricks go in another entrance with women – but you know that.
You'll pick it up easily again. Once learnt, hard to forget.
You've both certainly had so much experience with me.
Hey – if you don't marry - adopt a wife.

ALAN

Not necessary.

PATRICIA

What? You have both got wives already? Each other?

It is becoming become dark outside and there is the sound of distant thunder.

PATRICIA

It sounds like a thunderstorm. I had better be going.

ALAN

What?

MICHAEL

It's Sunday.

PATRICIA

You going to bring God into this again?
Trains and planes run on Sundays.
But the thunderstorm looks worrying.
You know our luck with thunderstorms?
Presage great things or bad things – certainly presage change of some sort.

MICHAEL

You are not really going?

PATRICIA

There's a plane at nine tonight.

ALAN

What?

PATRICIA

I would certainly like to be on it.

MICHAEL

Adoption papers?

PATRICIA

Adoption papers? Are you serious?
You are their dads - do you need adoption papers?

ALAN
My God she could be serious.

PATRICIA
Very serious.
My heavy suitcases are with the porter. Took
them down lunchtime.

ALAN
But it's irresponsible.

PATRICIA
They are fed and milked and watered and have
clean nappies.
You can stay here for another 24 hours.
Then they'll escort you off the premises.
I always thought that was funny – seeing the
nurses put you in taxi, holding your head in
case you bump yourself - like detectives with
the villain getting into the police car.
The hospital has responsibility until the car door
slams and you've left the hospital grounds,
And then the hospital is free of all
responsibility for your child – children – for
evermore.
Bit like me when the taxi door slams.
Goodbye Michael.
Goodbye Alan.
Goodbye children.
Have a happy life.
Oh! I found this.

From her handbag - she takes out the plastic policeman
she first saw in Alan's supermarket basket.

PATRICIA
I found it in my handbag the other day – whilst
I was clearing out.

I have no use for it. Do you want it back?
I remember you said you had it to keep yourself
in order.
Does that still apply?
Perhaps if you have no more use for it you can
eventually pass it on to the children.
They ought to know about policemen soon
enough.
Did you ever give it a name?
And what are you going to call them?
I'll leave you to decide.
It's none of my business.
But be sensible. Nothing fancy.

Do you have an umbrella?
Perhaps they can give me one downstairs.
Hey - I can hear the thunder getting closer - I
had better get going.
See you ......
No - sorry - wrong thing to say.
I don't imagine I will ever see you or them ever
again.
Jesus I am going to get wet

Bye.

SECTION 40

HOSPITAL ENTRANCE – DEPARTURE
Day. Interior. Thunderstorm. Spring.

Hospital entrance. Accompanied by a hospital-porter carrying her two suitcases, Patricia looks out from the hospital porch– thunder approaching – thunder-lightning lights up her face. Starting to rain. She puts up an umbrella. A taxi arrives with its lights on – it's getting late afternoon dark.
The porter puts the two suitcases into the trunk of the taxi. Patricia steps through the heavy rain.

Alan and Michael - expressionless - noses pressed to the window – are watching the rain - from the hospital second floor. Hospital lights go on behind them.

Patricia – wet with the heavy rain - gets into the taxi – shows a length of attractive leg. Arranges herself on the back seat.

Taxi drives off – rain starts to pour. Patricia doesn't look back.

The men have disappeared from the hospital window. Alan's plastic policeman is balanced on a cross-piece of the window fenestration. We see the plastic figure against lightning in the dark sky.

The Heavens open – thunder and lightning.
Rain lashing down on the hospital tarmac.
Huge storm on hospital frontage.
White water bouncing on the tarmac – "steel pins and silver rings".

End credit sequence with colossal thunderstorm over the hospital, the hospital grounds, the street, the city - with the occasional sound of two distressed one-day old babies on the soundtrack – super the end credits.

THE END